# Student Organization Leadership

**Starting, Running, and Improving a Student Group**

*Second Edition*
*Expanded and Revised*

Cyrus Fakharzadeh, MS, PMP
Mark Todd, PhD

ISBN  0-7414-5737-7

*Published by:*

**INFI∞ITY**
PUBLISHING.COM

*1094 New DeHaven Street, Suite 100*
*West Conshohocken, PA 19428-2713*
*Info@buybooksontheweb.com*
*www.buybooksontheweb.com*
*Toll-free  (877) BUY BOOK*
*Local Phone (610) 941-9999*
*Fax  (610) 941-9959*

*Printed in the United States of America*

*Published January 2010*

# Contents

Preface 1

Acknowledgements 3

## Chapter 1
How to Form and Lead a Student Group 5
Motivation for Being a Student Leader 5
Starting Your Own Student Group 8
Types of Organizations 8
Researching Other Organizations 8
Naming an Organization 9
Recognition of an Organization 9
Role of an Advisor 9
Team Size 10
Recruiting Board or Committee Members 10
Assigning Roles 12
Staff Members 13
Motivating Your Team 14
Setting a Vision 14
Conflicts of Interest and Time 15
Facilitating Success 15
Running for Office in an Existing Student Organization 16

## Chapter 2
How to Lead a Committee, Board, and Senate Meeting 19
Writing an Agenda 19
Running a Committee Meeting 22
Running a Board Meeting 23
Running a Senate Meeting 25

## Chapter 3
How to Write or Revise the Constitution and Bylaws 29
Overview of Constitution and Bylaws 29
Writing the Constitution and Bylaws 29
Content of a Constitution 31
Content of the Bylaws 33
Enforcement of the Constitution and Bylaws 34
Revising the Constitution and Bylaws 35

Epitome                                                          36

## Chapter 4

## How to Manage Budgeting, Financing, and Purchasing   37
Why Pay a Membership or Programming Fee?                  37
Setting the Budget                                       38
Above-the-line Income and Expenses                       39
Expenditures                                             40
The Cost of Student Government                            41
Board Programming                                        42
Senate Programming                                       42
Adjustments to the Budget                                43
Requesting Money                                         45
Approving Finance Requests                               45
Disbursing Funds                                         46
Buying                                                   47

## Chapter 5

## How to Promote and Publicize an Organization           51
Why Promote and Publicize?                               51
Establishing a Web site and E-mail Accounts              51
Creating and Distributing Brochures and Flyers           53
Purchasing and Distributing Promotional Items            54
Tabling                                                  55
Speaking at Orientation or Other Events                  55
Creating a Mailing List                                  55
Other Advertising Strategies                             56
Offering Food and Drinks                                 57
Holding a General Meeting                                59
Recap                                                    61

## Chapter 6

## How to Organize and Coordinate Programs                63
Why Program?                                             63
Program Planning                                         63
Publicizing Your Programs                                67
Selling Tickets for Events                               67
Serving Food and Drinks                                  68
Choosing a Venue                                         69
Event Management                                         70

Organizing a Conference 71
Debriefing 74

## Chapter 7

## How to Get Feedback and Address Issues of Members 75

Purpose of Student Advocacy 75
Forming Committees 75
Writing a Survey 77
Administering a Survey 78
Rewards as Incentives 78
Data Analysis 79
Making a Report 79
Approving Recommendations 82
Circulating the Report 82
Collaborating with the Administration on a Large Survey 82

## Chapter 8

## How to Relate to and Negotiate with Administrators 85

10 Tips for Success with Administrators 85
Tip 1: Converse with the Top of the Totem Pole 86
Tip 2: Know What You Want to Accomplish
and How They Can Help 86
Tip 3: Dress Appropriately 87
Tip 4: Arrange for a Meeting 88
Tip 5: Be Nice 88
Tip 6: Ask for Help in Private 89
Tip 7: Work Hard and Delegate When You Can 89
Tip 8: Dream Big and
Don't be Deterred by the Fear of Failure 90
Tip 9: Say "Thank you" in Public 92
Tip 10: Keep Yourself Continually in Their Thoughts 93

## Chapter 9

## How to Carry Out Elections, Transitions, and Training 95

Elections 95
Preparing for the Election 96
Running an Election 97
Transition Meetings 99
Training New Officers 102
Documenting Officers' Roles 102

Officer and Committee Reports 103
Recognizing Achievements 104

Chapter 10
How to Improve or
Turn Around a Student Organization 107
Overview of the Improvement Process 107
Forming a Task Force 111
Improving Morale and Performance 111
Demoting vs. Dismissing Board Members 111
Resigning from Office 112
Running a Special Election 113
Restructuring an Organization 113
Transforming an Organization 113
Changing the Advisor 114
Conclusion 115

Appendix A: Sample Constitution 117

Appendix B: Sample Bylaws 121

Appendix C: Sample Agendas 127

Appendix D: Time Matrix 129

Appendix E: Sample Funding Request Form 131

Appendix F: Sample Member Survey 133

Appendix G: Sample Memorandum 137

Appendix H: Sample Departmental Survey 139

Appendix I: Sample Board Survey 141

References 143

Index 145

About the Authors 153
Biography of Cyrus Fakharzadeh 153
Biography of Mark Todd 153

# Preface

Student organization leadership can be defined as follows: the act of leading an organization of students that may be represented as an assembly, an association, a body, a class (e.g., sophomore, junior, or senior), a club, a committee, a council, a government, a group, or a society.

Intended as a resource for leaders of student groups, this book is the result of years of collaboration and writing from authors who have a number of years of experience successfully leading student organizations. Much of what we have proposed includes ideas and approaches that we have found to be successful in our own leadership experience and successful for other organizations we have advised. Our mission is to assist students in becoming better leaders and help maximize the effectiveness of student organizations.

The heuristic challenge in writing a book on student organizations is that student leadership is more of an art than a science. Therefore, we have focused on ten areas of student organization leadership that form the chapters of this book. We address five major constraints of student organizations: limited advisement, budget, personnel, participation, and training. This book aims to help solve these problems faced by student leaders with their demanding academic workloads.

Although the responsibilities of leading a committee may differ from those of leading a student government, many of the principles are the same. Thus, the privilege of leadership should be assumed with a commitment to acquiring the tools that enable the leader to be as effective as possible. This book is written for student leaders of all levels of responsibility and experience. Whether you are chair of a committee, an officer or board member of a student organization, or part of the student government leadership this book should help you become a more effective leader.

This second edition has been revised and updated to include a new chapter on *How to Improve or Turn around a Student Organization*, based on an improvement process and the steps to follow for solving organizational problems.

Computer files associated with portions of the book are also available. These tools help users in recreating the relevant documents and tables from the text to apply to their own organizations. To find more information about these resources and student organization leadership, please visit our Web site at **www.studentorgleader.com**.

Student organizations play a critical role in the life of students and the caliber of the leadership can have dramatic effects on the success of the group. Our experiences as student leaders would have been much better if we had a book like this to read before we began running our student organizations. Fundamentally, we hope that you gain insight by reading this book and that it helps you achieve success in your leadership role.

# Acknowledgements

We express gratitude to all of those who helped us in making this book possible. In particular, we are grateful to the many individuals, administrators, and advisors who contributed by their own involvement and support of the organizations that we served.

The institutions, particularly the University of Southern California, where we were students deserve much credit for providing the structure and culture within which we served as student leaders in the Graduate and Professional Student Senate and other organizations. The experiences we had as leaders of student groups, governments, and committees were crucial in contributing to the content of our book.

We especially thank our parents, families, and friends who have helped us throughout our lives in so many ways, and we dedicate this book to them.

Ultimately, our mission is to assist student leaders, advisors, and organizations by helping them to be as effective as possible. Accordingly, we remain committed to continuously improving the quality of this publication. Therefore, we encourage our readers to let us know their comments and recommendations about this book by contacting us directly by e-mail at book@studentorgleader.com. Thank you!

# Chapter 1

## How to Form and Lead a Student Group

### Motivation for Being a Student Leader

Being a leader of a student group is the ideal setting for you to grow and gain experience in leadership. Academic institutions take their students very seriously and whenever a student group is formed, the institutions embrace it and permit it to function as part of the family of student organizations, as long as the organization and its officers are in compliance with the policies of the institution. There are many opportunities for leadership at the student level, and the institution welcomes new leaders recognizing that there will be lessons learned in the crucible of student groups that cannot be gathered from the formal classroom setting. The arena of student leadership is somewhat public, and the stakes are high enough to warrant careful attention to all aspects of leadership. While exemplary leaders are lauded, unethical conduct and egregious abuse of the leadership privilege can result in severe sanctions for violating the student conduct code. Few leaders are remembered beyond their term of leadership, but the benefits of an effective leader to the student body and even to an institution will remain for many years.

You may be considering whether or not you could be a student leader. Indeed, there are several reasons for becoming a student leader, among them are the following listed below.

1. *Leadership Training*: You will have the opportunity to develop your leadership abilities in a setting where you can learn without risking your job and income. While the stakes are not as high as they would be in a job, you are nevertheless developing your leadership skills in a public setting.

2. *Improving Knowledge*: Student groups are a great way for you to learn more and broaden your awareness of other aspects of your field and interests. You will learn things that are not traditionally taught in academic courses and possibly gain insight into the way academic institutions function.

3. *Improving Communication Skills*: You will enhance your communication skills by making many different types of presentations and by public speaking in both prepared and extemporaneous styles. Written communication skills will be developed through writing the many e-mails and documents that are the responsibility of a student leader.

Strong written and oral communication skills are among the most commonly mentioned requirements in job descriptions, and you will have an advantage over your peers in the job application process as a result of your student leadership experience.

4. *Networking*: You will have the opportunity to build relationships with other students and with school administrators which could result in valuable leads or referrals for employment. At the same time, you will develop your social skills and character in building lasting friendships and relationships with others.

5. *Resume Building*: Being a student leader will impress potential employers and set you apart from those who have not held leadership positions. However, the experience gained is really only valuable if your student group is active and making a difference to your fellow students. In the public setting of student leadership, the difference between being a leader and merely holding a leadership position will determine the experience you accumulate and the respect you earn from your peers and those administrators, from whom you may be seeking a letter of recommendation for a job in the future.

There are also some drawbacks to being a student leader including the following listed below.

1. *Less Free Time*: Since you will spend considerable time on the student group, especially if you want to be successful, you will have less time for socializing with your friends. You will have many meetings, training sessions, events to plan and attend, and phone calls to make that all take away your free time. This is the time that your peers will spend having fun, going out, or relaxing. Developing time management and multitasking skills will help you find the right balance between work, study, and play, enabling you to get the most out of your student experience. Leading an organization is not for everyone, especially not for those without enough time to devote to the group.

2. *Excess Work*: You will have to take on added responsibilities and deal with a number of problems encountered by student leaders. Often, people will let you down, vendors will run short of supplies, plans will change, money will run out, and you, as the leader, will bear the responsibility of maintaining a smooth running organization in the face of all these challenges. You will have to learn how to prioritize and develop useful management and problem-solving skills, if you want to avoid burnout. Most importantly, you must maintain satisfactory grades in your academic pursuit and avoid the temptation of putting student group work before your studies.

3. *Stress*: It might sound strange, but you may lose sleep worrying about your student group. You will likely have to deal with difficult situations that will test your patience and ability to work well under pressure. You will have to deal with difficult people, inclement weather, under-attended events, failure of initiatives, and many other things that go wrong. As a leader, you will learn how to deal with uncertainty and chaos and develop your organizational abilities.

4. *Communication Overload*: You will likely get inundated by e-mails and letters that demand your immediate attention. Student leaders can get hundreds of e-mails to read and to reply to. They can even get a high number of phone calls and text or voice messages. All of this frequent communication can take up a lot of time and test your ability to prioritize.

5. *Ethical Dilemmas*: You may be faced with situations where friends will ask for personal favors or preferential treatment, or where you may be offered preferential treatment because of your position. This is a big challenge to leaders in all arenas of life, and your reputation could be tarnished by making even a small unethical decision. You will have to learn to put the interests of your organization before the interests of anyone involved with the group. As a leader who consistently makes ethical decisions, you will gain the respect of the wider academic community and elevate the status of your organization in the process.

The bottom line before you start is to make sure that you are ready for such a commitment. Being a student leader means that you need to have or make the time to run a student group effectively. If you are too busy and really have no free time, then you should think about whether you are ready to dive into this rare experience of a lifetime. The skills you will gain from starting a student group or from being a student leader will make you a more marketable candidate for future jobs you may seek. You will develop your character in the process and become better-rounded as a student and as an individual. However, the primary motivation of a leader should be to help drive the organization forward, and not primarily to add a line on a resume or for the sole purpose of elevating one's standing within the student body. Even if you are not sure about whether to start a student group or become a student leader, you will gain valuable insight into the amount of work you would be expected to do by reading this book.

## Starting Your Own Student Group

Student groups, when run well, are very effective vehicles of advocacy and community building in academic institutions. They are formed within a rich and constantly changing environment of diversity, interdisciplinarity, and diversion from academic pursuit. They can address the needs of the student body representing the entire cohort, in the case of student government, or a few students with eclectic interests. As a leader of a student group, you will have an insight into the academic administration and a responsibility for meeting the needs of a group of students, whether large or small. Whether you form a new group or become a leader in an established organization, the achievements and challenges you will experience as a student leader will serve you well after you graduate and into the next phase of your life.

## Types of Organizations

There are a number of different types of student organizations including:
- Academic
- Cultural
- Fraternal
- Governing
- International
- Political
- Recreational
- Religious
- Social
- Special Interest

More than one classification may apply to an organization, such as those that act as student governments at the class, departmental, school, or college level.

## Researching Other Organizations

The first thing to do when starting a student group is to check that your proposed organization or chapter does not already exist at your school. Try doing searches on the Web for groups similar to your own. If it does not exist at your school, you will likely find organizations or chapters under a similar name at different schools, which will give you ideas on their composition, activities, and goals. This can save you a lot of time in trying to figure what you need to do to start your own organization.

If you are starting a chapter of a national or international organization, you should seek help from the local chapter. If there is no local representation you may not have adequate support during your chapter formation, and the chapter may not have the structure to outlive your leadership once you graduate.

## Naming an Organization

If you are forming a student chapter, the name of your school would typically precede the name of the corresponding larger national or international organization. If you are forming a new organization with no chapter affiliation, then you will need to decide on a name that fits the nature of your group, membership, department, or school. Keep in mind that the acronym that represents the abbreviation of your organization should not have any negative connotations or suggest anything offensive or profane.

## Recognition of an Organization

Many institutions require a formal set of procedures to follow when starting an organization or registering the group annually. Check with your institution for the specific process that is to be followed. For instance, you may have to fill out a form and submit a copy of your constitution and bylaws and agree to strictly abide by school policies.

If you are forming a chapter, you may also have to apply for annual membership renewal or recognition with your national society. Check the Web site of the national organization to which your chapter belongs to determine any specific requirements for chartering or renewal. Having your student group officially recognized, by your institution and chapter, affords you the opportunity to partake in the rich array of student-led organizations and governments and to make an impact on the academic community whose interests you represent.

## Role of an Advisor

Typically, you will need a faculty or staff member to serve as an advisor to your organization. In the case of student governments, one may even be assigned by the school. The advisor should be approachable and have the time to discuss organizational matters with you. Having an advisor with previous experience advising organizations, particularly related to your own, is very helpful. If the advisor is a former board member or officer of your organization, then the advisor could provide expertise and knowledge that would enrich the group and enhance your leadership experience.

Communicating with advisors regularly is recommended either in person or by e-mail. Keep them informed of the happenings of the organization and any outstanding issues or problems you need to resolve. The more they know about the organization, the better assistance they can provide to you and your successors, because they will probably still be advising your organization after you have graduated or ended your tenure as a leader. A more involved advisor is needed for organizations with less experienced leaders and those who need more help with complex issues. However, they should not interfere with your leadership. If you find that your advisor is not contributing much, is consistently unavailable, or is causing other problems, then you should consider finding another one.

## Team Size

The size of your board depends upon such factors as the scale of your organization and number of members. The boards of student governments can consist of over ten members, while the boards of typical organizations consist of as few as four or five members. Having more board members or officers does not necessarily mean the organization will be better and the more team members you have, the more you will have to train and manage them. There are also communication issues associated with having more board members, and larger boards tend to have more difficulty in finding times when they can meet. Having too many positions on the board may be difficult to fill, so you should adjust the size of your board to meet the needs of your organization. Remember, you can always have more people serving as committee chairs or members responsible for particular aspects of the organization without having them serve as officers.

For student governments or large department/school organizations, a senate may be formed with representatives from individual departments or schools. The number of senators for each department or school should be proportional to the number of students in their respective departments or schools.

## Recruiting Board or Committee Members

In the early stages of forming a student group, you will need to choose a team to serve as members of your board. It is advisable to look beyond your immediate circle of friends, because you want to avoid your organization becoming a clique. Even your best friends can disappoint you, if they are not willing to put as much effort into the organization as you are. They may take advantage of your friendship and do less for you than someone you do not know very well, and your relationship may suffer if you try to hold them to your level of expectation and dedication. When choosing your board you should ideally base your decision on more than just an interview. Interviews only reveal the impression one makes on another, and there are a lot of things that you will not know about a person through a short interview. You really need to test your potential candidates by observing their dedication to your organization in a volunteer capacity. Finding out how they performed in other student groups will also help you decide whether they will be an asset to your organization.

In general, there are three main groups of people who associate themselves with student groups:

1. *Contributors* (those who help an organization)
2. *Slackers* (those who do little or nothing for an organization)
3. *Troublemakers* (those who harm an organization)

There may be degrees within each of these groups and some people may be inconsistent, vacillating between these categories at different times, depending on their mood, their academic workload, personality conflicts, or leadership decisions that they do not like. It is difficult to predict which category people will fall into, especially when you do not know them very well.

It should go without saying that all your officers should be in adequate academic standing with satisfactory grades and without any student conduct violations. As a student, academics should be the first priority, and you do not want to be in the position of having any officers unable to perform their duties, because they are spending all their time trying to rescue their GPA in order to graduate. Students with academic conduct violations may not have the ethical predisposition you will need in order for your organization to remain in compliance with the institutional policies. You should also try to recruit a diverse group of board members representing different genders, races, ages, and academic affiliation, if appropriate. Diversity can help in attracting more members and will likely help in recruiting other students for roles on committees and as successors to the existing leadership.

Your officers should be available through an entire academic year. For example, they should not plan to take a term studying abroad or hold an internship which would take them away from campus and thus remove them from the day-to-day operations of the organization. Your officers should also be aware of the expectations of holding the position prior to assuming their role. They should either have the time or be prepared to make time for the work, and if not, then they should not be considered.

There are four major qualities that are essential in potential board members. These students should be:

1. *Capable* (are qualified and have the time to commit to the organization)
2. *Willing* (have the will and determination to do the work)
3. *Dependable* (will do the work reliably and with minimal oversight)

4. *Ethical* (will not compromise the integrity of the organization)

Your officers need to be able to do their job reliably without being micromanaged. Managing and micromanaging people consumes a lot of time. You can't afford to have officers who are slackers and who willingly delegate tasks while doing little or nothing themselves. This can have detrimental effects on the morale of your volunteers and members. Student groups are not for selfish people. You should recruit students who are effective in group settings, team players who get along with others, and are willing to put the needs of the organization before any personal agenda. Do not be afraid to recruit students who might be even more experienced than you or have a more successful track record as a leader. They can bring success to your organization and you can learn a lot from them.

Ideally, student leaders should be active and involved in an organization for a year or at least a term (e.g., quarter or semester) before becoming an officer, and when forming a new student group, prior involvement in a different organization will help. If officers on the board don't care about doing their job well, the organization may never gather any momentum. If you are lucky, you will be able to assemble a core set of experienced officers in your most critical positions who will perform as a team. For any leadership position, an active member serving on a committee or a senator in the student government may have the potential to be a successful officer, and the more open you are to consider a variety of candidates, the better your chances of selecting a great board for your organization.

## Assigning Roles

At a minimum your board will need a president and officers responsible for programs, finance, and communication. These positions are associated with the major functions of a student group. You may also wish to have an executive vice president or chief-of-staff depending on the size of your board. As the organization becomes more established and assumes a greater mandate, more positions may be added as needed. Assigning titles to these board positions should be done thoughtfully, and whether the officer responsible for the budget is called a Vice President·of Finance or the Chair of the Finance Committee will depend on how your organization is structured. If the majority of your work is done through committees and the chairs of those committees form the executive officers or board of the organization, then the title of Finance Chair or a similar derivative may be appropriate. However, some consider that the title of Vice President looks better on a resume and denotes a more professionally structured organization.

Ideal candidates for the position of president need to be self-motivated and effective leaders, preferably with experience as a vice president in the organization or as president in another student group. They need to be able to direct operations, uphold expectations, set the example of hard work and ethical conduct, and oversee the work of others. For a vice president of finance, an ideal candidate should have experience as a finance officer in another organization or should have served on a finance committee. They should also be people with integrity who will abide by the rules that govern disbursement of money as laid out by your institution. Students with backgrounds in the fields of business, accounting, or economics are fitting candidates to consider even in the absence of formal involvement in a student group. For a vice president of programs, an ideal candidate should have experience in a similar role from another organization or have served as a member of an activities/events committee or a programming committee. It should be a person with a passion for academic and social programs who enjoys interacting with students, vendors, and school officials and is skillful at organizing events. For a vice president of communication, an ideal candidate should have the capability of creating a listserv or mail list and Web sites. They should be able to write well and avoid causing embarrassment to your organization through spelling errors in e-mails or on Web sites. An executive vice president or chief-of-staff can help with keeping the other officers on track and following up with them, allowing the president to focus on advocacy or other issues. Having co-presidents, however, is likely to cause conflicts and lead to problems in reaching final agreements and decisions and, therefore, should be avoided.

## Staff Members

Particularly for student government, having paid staff and even paid board members is not unusual. Running a student government is a huge responsibility and requires a lot of administrative support. It is in the interests of the student body, and to some extent of the institution, that the student government is run well. Therefore, in some cases a paid staff member and/or student workers are required to keep the office open and running smoothly. Student government work, when done well is equivalent to a part-time job. Tuition remission or a stipend can be awarded to officers with the amount depending on the role and responsibility of the position and the budget available. The concern with any paid student group or government position is that people will become involved primarily for the remuneration, rather than because of a passion for the organization or for student issues. There should be a provision in your constitution for removal of an officer who is not working hard enough to merit the remuneration. For organizations that are not student governments, paid board or staff members are not usually required in order to have a successful group.

## Motivating Your Team

Issuing threats and coercion are usually not the best ways to motivate your team. Be careful not to be perceived as intimidating, and do not harass or overburden your officers and volunteers. You should lead by example setting the expectations and standard for others to follow. Motivate others by building rapport and networking effectively with them. Projecting a winning attitude and rewarding those for excellence by giving awards and recognition during or at the end of the academic year will serve as an incentive to encourage your team to perform well. Unlike the business world where stress is high and firings are common, student organizations are concerned, not with profit, but with increasing membership, advancing student issues, and improving student life.

Those who do well in volunteer settings will feel a reward for doing a great job, seeing your efforts bear fruit, and gaining experience and new friends in the process. The challenge in leading a group of volunteers is to motivate them. Most volunteers in student groups are passionate about their issues and their motivation is largely intrinsic. Sometimes there can be tension between paid officers and volunteers. As a student leader, you need to make sure that the work is distributed appropriately between those who are paid and those who are volunteers. You should be careful not to take advantage of willing volunteers to avoid their burnout or disenchantment with the organization.

There are a number of team-building exercises that you can do to motivate your team. You can socialize together by playing a board game or sport, go to the beach or park, or go out to the movies or for a meal. Any activity that involves teamwork is a great way to develop a cooperative team spirit among your board members and volunteers. A divisive team, on the other hand, is characterized by jealousy, selfishness, and an overly competitive spirit that will ruin your organization's chances of being effective.

## Setting a Vision

As a leader of an organization, you need to define the goals for your year in office. The vision you lay out should be supported by your board and should serve the group and its members. There may be some disagreement on the specifics of how to achieve certain goals, but a clear vision to make the organization successful should be communicated to your team. While you can anticipate a degree of uncertainty, you need to have some flexibility to adjust to possible changes in how you accomplish your vision. While having a vision is essential for success, you need to work hard on bringing those ideas and the vision to fruition.

## Conflicts of Interest and Time

It is inadvisable to be an officer of more than one organization at the same time. You could have trouble deciding on where you need to spend your time and energy or deciding which organization takes priority, when faced with two simultaneous decisions or events. While there may be a case where one organization is complimentary with another, and serving in a position with one group can help the other one, holding a position of responsibility in more than one organization will consume too much of your time, especially if you aim to do a worthwhile job as a student leader. A real potential conflict of interest would be serving as an officer in an organization that governs another one in which you are also an officer. The old saying about not playing first and second base at the same time holds true.

Having romantic relationships with board members, committee members, and other members of the organization may also lead to conflicts of interest. Relationships can be difficult to conceal from the public eye, and there may be accusations of preferential treatment directed towards you by other members of your organization. Moreover, there may be difficulties in holding such partners accountable, when they do not do what they are supposed to do for the organization. Also, the possibility of a breakup of a romantic relationship could severely damage crucial communication links. It is therefore advisable to wait until the end of your term before pursuing a serious, personal relationship with anyone on your board or committee.

## Facilitating Success

While the success of an organization is largely dependent on the leadership and volunteers, there are other accommodations that will greatly help your group function efficiently. If possible, you should check whether your school can provide your group with office space, even if you have to share with another organization. This can help if there is a need to have a place for meeting and storage. Office furniture, file cabinets, desks, telephones, computers, printers, a copier, and a fax machine are great to have in an office. Office hours for you and your board members can be established to improve communication. If this is not possible or the space is not large enough to hold your board, it may be possible to reserve conference or meeting rooms in your school or department. Mail slots for the organization, board members, senators, and committees can also greatly improve communication.

A storage space or closet that is secured can help with storing equipment and supplies needed for your organization. You may need to purchase a cart to help with hauling equipment around, and plastic buckets may even be needed to store food and drinks. You should take inventory of the possessions of your organization and keep track of where things are going, so that you do not lose them. To help with tracking the supplies, food, and drinks you have in storage you can use an Excel spreadsheet that is regularly updated.

If possible, establish school e-mail accounts for the organization, board members, and committees. That way, if an officer or committee chair is not able to check e-mail, another officer can log into the e-mail account and continue with the issues at hand. It also permits greater continuity between board members or committee chairs when new leadership transitions into the organization.

## Running for Office in an Existing Student Organization

In deciding whether or not to join an organization that already exists, you should first determine whether the group will be around in the future or whether it will be short-lived. Some groups are spawned in response to a perceived need or issue and do not outlive the resolution of the issue, while other organizations are formed less impulsively and serve the needs of an established student cohort for years. The organization's reputation and history will determine its longevity and consequently the effect your hard work will have on future generations of students, if you decide to get involved.

It is recommended to get involved as soon as you are ready in your student life. By starting early, you will benefit from having more years of association with the organization and gain valuable experience in the way it is run with successive leaders. Joining a committee will help you become more familiar with the organization and the role of the officers, and you will be able to test your compatibility with the group. You will also gain valuable training and leadership experience, enabling you to assume more responsibility as the officers gain confidence in your ability and commitment. If you have ambitions for joining the board of an existing organization, you may have to run for office. A position as a president, vice president, or committee chair offers an incomparable opportunity to serve your organization and its members. Although you assume more responsibility, authority, and prestige, you will be expected to know more and be able to mentor others within the organization. For this reason, the best leaders tend to be the ones who have been involved in the organization at the volunteer or committee level, having demonstrated commitment and gained understanding and experience to be a more effective leader.

To declare your candidacy for an election, you may be required to file your intent to run for office by submitting an application. Make sure that you meet all requirements and deadlines for filing. You may even be required to submit a statement of purpose with highlights of your background, qualifications, and goals to convince others that you should be elected. If you are not a great campaigner, you might want to look for open and unopposed positions in organizations that interest you as a way to become a student leader.

You may have to run a campaign to be elected for certain organizations, especially student governments. If you are running for president, you may have to select a vice president as a running mate. Choosing your running mate should be strategic. You should choose someone who is strong in areas where you are weak or inexperienced and complements your skills and abilities. Make sure your running mate has a similar vision for the organization and that you are both going to be able to work effectively together. Running mates should be of high moral character and able to place the interests of the organization above their own.

To help with your campaign, you can recruit a staff and appoint a campaign director. Make sure that you and your staff comply with all school policies and do not violate any campaign rules. Sanctions for breaching campaign rules can range from suspension of campaigning privileges for a period of time to disqualification. You should develop a campaign budget and determine your funding options. If permissible, you may be able to accept financial contributions and donations. Keep your expenditures as low as possible, since overspending will lead to incurred debt, and no organization really wants leaders who cannot manage their finances.

You will need to develop a winning campaign platform that addresses the needs of the student cohort that will be voting. You may have to develop campaign slogans, posters, stickers, signs, and pamphlets to highlight your background, qualifications, accomplishments, contributions, and goals. If appropriate, you will need to delegate distribution and posting of campaign materials to others. Make sure that you comply with all school policies on posting, and do not offend anyone with the content. Since much of success is based on popularity and being well known, you may even want to establish a Web site to promote your candidacy. You should meet with your constituents to determine what issues matter to them, and you should build your campaign around those issues. As you meet your constituents, you should use the opportunity to garner their support by assuring them that you will do all you can to address their issues. You may have to deliver a campaign speech in public or maybe even participate in debates between candidates and/or meetings with voters. Therefore, it is important to practice speaking in front of others or have your campaign staff pose challenging questions for you to answer. If you are elected, be prepared to address your supporters with an acceptance speech.

Becoming involved with an established organization or starting your own student group will enrich your student life. If you manage your time well, you should be able to enjoy a balanced student experience with purposeful academic, social, and leadership pursuits. You will leave the student life having gained leadership experience and having made a difference to a portion of the student body, and you will consider the time devoted to your organization as time well spent.

# Chapter 2

## How to Lead a Committee, Board, and Senate Meeting

### Writing an Agenda

A well-planned agenda is crucial to an orderly meeting. While simply having an agenda keeps everyone on track, a smart board or committee will have little tolerance for an unsubstantial agenda. An effective agenda must consist of important and essential items that merit the attention of an ambitious group of elected student leaders. For organizations that are being started for the first time and those that are beginning their new terms, the first meeting sets an important tone for the new academic year.

The agenda needs to be strategically prepared in line with the goals for the year and should never be something you think of simply week-by-week. There are only so many meetings in the year, and you will have to stagger the issues you consider at the meetings, because you cannot possibly deal with all issues every week. You should try to set out a whole year's worth of major agenda items so that they all get covered and then, as different issues come up, you can focus on the specifics of each meeting and include smaller agenda items as they arise. Sometimes the goals have to be achieved by a certain deadline and that will set the priority. For example, when coordinating with administrators, especially when printed materials are involved, there are often deadlines that they have to meet and, if you want to partner with them, you will be held to those deadlines also. Initiatives which require significant changes to school policy or practice usually take much longer, are not realized until the following year, and require many months of hard work. A thoughtful strategic approach means that you can space out your time-consuming agenda items and initiatives to permit maximum attention, rather than having two or three concurrent big items with less time and attention to devote to them. In planning the meeting agendas for the year, you should think of the initiatives you have identified in your goals and try to predict which ones will take the longest to bring to fruition. You should then place them in order and address the ones that will take almost a whole year to realize at your early meetings, so that the ensuing committees can begin work on them right away. Initiatives that may take as little as a month to realize can be addressed mid to late in the year, in order to accomplish as many of the goals outlined in your vision as possible.

It is important to circulate the agenda prior to the meeting. You should put out a call for agenda items to the board or committee members with a firm deadline for response. Officers who miss that deadline will have to address their items during the "any other business" section of the agenda, usually at the end of the meeting if time permits. As soon after the deadline as you can, you should circulate the agenda to allow officers to prepare their thoughts on items that their colleagues wish to discuss. This reinforces the deadline and gives maximum time for officers to prepare for the meeting. It is also essential to bring hard copies of the agenda to the meeting, though some may wish to use the electronic version on their laptop computers and make notes against each item during the discussion. Some general items on an agenda are discussed in the following pages.

## Call to Order

Each meeting should begin with a call to order, and the time that the call to order is made should be recorded by the person taking the minutes. It is very important to call the meeting to order at the time the meeting is scheduled to start, even if not all members are present. This sets a tone and usually the stragglers will arrive in better time for future meetings.

## Approving the Minutes

The second item on an agenda is usually an official approval of the minutes of the previous meeting. Here you will ask the committee to read and make amendments to the minutes of the previous meeting and then vote to ratify their accuracy. This is very important, because it is essential that you document and agree on what was discussed, so that a permanent record can be created and you can show your constituents that you have been conducting serious business on their behalf in your meetings. If you invite administrators to your meetings, it is essential to make notes of the key points of their presentation and include them in the minutes. If you ever have the occasion to advocate with administrators who may have forgotten the particular promise made during one of your meetings, you will be able to present them with a copy of the approved minutes reminding them of their promise. In this way, approving the minutes serves as a powerful tool for holding people accountable to their responsibilities and reinforces the professional image your organization needs to uphold in the academic environment.

## New Business

New business can be anything that does not fall under officer reports later in the agenda. It usually pertains to big issues that involve the whole board or committee, rather than an item that falls within the purview of a certain officer or sub-committee. In student government, finance requests are frequently addressed under this heading since new requests are typically made each week and require the input and vote of all committee members. The agenda is an overview of the meeting and additional materials required for a presentation should be available for committee members, in order to assist with understanding specific agenda items, especially new business items. For example, your finance committee or officer should review the finance requests and prepare a summary sheet for each board or committee member with the requested amount, name of the organization, fund from which the money was requested, and justification and breakdown of the request. Such information could not be included on the agenda and would detract from the purpose of the agenda, which is to guide the meeting and keep it on track. However, such additional information will facilitate the understanding of the members and significantly speed up the meeting.

### Officer Reports

This is where officers who submitted an agenda item by your deadline will appear with their agenda items listed below their name. This will include updates on initiatives or new ideas that the officer may be addressing. It is an opportunity for the rest of the committee to get acquainted with the work of the other officers and to ask questions or offer input. Officers are free to bring supplemental material to support their presentation, but only the item to be discussed should appear on the agenda beneath the officer's name and title.

### Any Other Business

Here is where items that officers forgot to list on the agenda or items of which they have just thought of can be addressed. This is also where the committee chair can ask officers to comment on the progress of an issue or initiative that the officers did not list among their agenda items. This section is also particularly useful if you only have one or two items each week deferred from the previous week. You can use this section of the agenda to follow up rather than create a separate deferred agenda.

### Calendar Updates/Breakout

In the rare event that a meeting finishes early, you might want to add a time for members to share their calendars with each other. Since the officers are already in the same room and expecting to stay for the duration of the meeting, you could also use the free time to break out into sub-committees that are working on issues together. Alternatively, you could use the extra time for an impromptu catch-up with other officers.

## Meeting Adjournment

Closing the meeting is as important as opening it. It is appropriate to thank the individuals for their time and their contributions to the meeting. The time of adjournment should be noted by the person who takes the minutes, and the meeting should end on time. This sets a tone of professionalism and honors the commitment you made with the members to let them leave by a certain time. In fact, if you need to extend a meeting you should stop the meeting at the appointed time to call for a vote to permit the meeting to continue. You should do this in blocks of fifteen minutes, voting to continue on each occasion.

## Running a Committee Meeting

Committees are convened to address specific issues of concern to the members. Committee meetings are the most informal meetings of an organization and may be held in conference rooms or classrooms that have been reserved in advance or, alternatively, conducted less formally at a table in a restaurant or cafeteria. A meeting announcement with the date, time, and location should be e-mailed to all members one week in advance, along with a reminder sent the day before the meeting. The committee chair should set and communicate a deadline for responding. Members should be encouraged never to miss meetings unless they have a justifiable reason (such as class, illness, injury, work, or other important reason), and they should let the chair know in advance.

The chair should try to arrive at least five minutes early, but never arrive late. While items can be discussed with one or two members present, voting cannot occur unless a quorum (majority of members present) has been reached. If the items being discussed require a vote, it is best to delay the discussion until the quorum is reached, otherwise you may have to repeat items.

Depending on the size of the committee, you may choose to follow Robert's Rules of Order (parliamentary law) as a guide, but typically committee meetings are not as structured as board meetings. The chair should try to avoid digression in the meetings by limiting conversations that deviate too much on topics unrelated to organizational matters. Items that are not relevant can be discussed before or after the meeting.

Depending on the issues and the magnitude of the tasks, the meeting frequency could vary from once every week to once every month during the academic year. Summer meetings may occur as needed if enough members are available. Committee minutes should be taken and either posted or filed electronically and reported back to the board for information.

## Running a Board Meeting

Leading a board meeting is probably the most important part of a student leader's role. The board is charged with the day-to-day running of the organization. Officers are typically smart and capable students who have a desire to succeed and bring about change to improve the quality of student life at the school. The number of officers will vary depending on the size of the student body and the philosophy of the organization. Typically, organizations have a president and an executive vice president who may be the chief-of-staff or may have a specific area of responsibility, depending on the size of the board. There will also typically be a vice president of finance, if there is a budget to be administered, and other officers with responsibility for social programming, academic programming, community service, communications, etc. The board is a powerful force, and when the board works as a cohesive unit, a great year of accomplishments is in store. These elected individuals will come with their own agendas, egos, and work ethics, and your job as a student leader is to harness this force and steer it towards a unity of purpose. To get all these bright and ambitious people in a room at the same time is to amass great potential, and to keep them coming back requires that the meetings be purposeful, structured, ethical, and focused on serving the constituency.

Running a board meeting requires some careful planning. Ideally, a day and time should be selected when all board members can attend that doesn't conflict with classes or work and gets them as near their best time as possible. Your meetings will probably be on a weekday after school for a couple of hours or until business is completed. If your organization has enough in the budget, it is a great idea to begin with food and, if you can, to plan a different vendor/selection each week for variety. For the board meeting where numbers are small, you should circulate a menu the week prior to the meeting so that officers can have their choice of food for the meeting. Beginning a meeting by serving food that the board or committee members have chosen for themselves makes for a satisfying start to the meeting. When a meal that people are looking forward to eating is delivered on time, such members have the extra incentive to arrive on time, and a meeting that starts on time is more likely to finish on time.

Time is an important issue in planning an agenda, and as the meeting progresses, people get more tired. With that in mind, you might want to change the order of officer reports each week, so that the same officer does not go last all the time and feel as if that person is constantly getting the least attention. No matter what your justification for the order of officer reports on the agenda, people almost always want to go first and mixing up the order has the effect of reducing any egotistical associations with a certain position on the agenda. You may even want to include the president's report in the alternating order each week. This helps officers to see that there is no implied seniority or importance to the agenda order.

During the board meeting, it is very important for all officers to feel that they have a voice on the board and that they are given a respectful environment and an appropriate amount of time in which to offer their thoughts. Often, there will be conflicting opinions and, as a leader, you need the tact to validate each officer's contribution without appearing to take sides or appear judgmental. Disagreement and discussion can be very healthy on a board if the meeting is consistently chaired well. The board meeting is usually where the problem-solving occurs and initiatives are fine-tuned, so that they can be presented to the senate for vote, if applicable. Sometimes the details can be tedious, and often committees will have done the groundwork and prepared the initiative for discussion at the board level. Time spent ironing out details and preparing thoroughly for the board meeting is time very well spent. If the officers know ahead of time, through a timely circulation of the agenda, they are more likely to be predisposed to a thoughtful and time-consuming discussion of a specific initiative at meeting time.

The board wields a lot of power in terms of the influence they have over the greater student body and the ability to allocate finances, as permitted by the constitution and bylaws of the organization. It is justifiable that boards are permitted to have authority over small but not insignificant amounts of money, whether it is in the form of an expense account or in the form of approving finance requests from student organizations. The board typically meets more frequently than the senate, and while the senate is the forum where large financial allocations to student groups should be made by majority vote, time is a factor and it makes sense for smaller amounts of money to be allocated by the board. Your organization may have a finance committee that meets weekly to review all requests less than a certain dollar amount and makes recommendations to the board. The requests and the finance committee's recommendations will be voted on or deferred pending clarification of the request.

It is in such situations of great responsibility, away from the scrutiny of the senate, that a student leader must remind the board that they are voting for the benefit of the organization, unlike senators who vote on behalf of their smaller constituents. Even officers have biases, and that is often reflected in the way one votes on a certain issue. The president probably won't have a vote in either the senate or board meeting except in a tie-breaking situation and, in such situations, the vote should be for the benefit of the membership.

The board is entrusted with providing the vision, budget, and direction for the year and while these may need to be passed with a majority vote by a senate, often the recommendations of officers carry significant weight. While a just senate will demand clear answers and justification before voting on an initiative, a tired and distracted senator will take the officer's opinion without much opposition. Thus, it is not unusual for the officers to be denied a vote in senate meetings. Often the board and the president drive the agenda for the senate meetings, and this agenda should reflect a broad and diverse array of items of interest to the senators and their constituents rather than just the items of interest to the board. In some schools, officers of student organizations may be compensated by a small amount of tuition remission or stipend that requires a return of a certain number of hours per week to be dedicated to student senate activities. As a result, officers have time to devote to issues that senators who are typically unpaid do not; this can also be good or bad depending on the officer. An ideal officer will be passionate about an issue, and indeed, may have been elected in part for that passionate resolve. It is tempting to spend one's time pursuing advocacy or programming about which one is passionate and an effective officer will do that well. However, outstanding officers will not only pursue the advocacy or programs about which they are passionate, they will also pursue with equal vigor issues or programs that cater to others of unlike minds who may even have voted against them. Therefore, a student leader needs to guard against filling the senate agenda only with initiatives that originate from within the board and issues for which the officers have a penchant.

## Running a Senate Meeting

One of the biggest challenges facing a student leader is to engage the members, especially those with whom there is a direct working relationship. This is the case in a senate where the senators are often required to attend the meetings amid a busy schedule of classes and study hours, more often than not, without any financial compensation. The student leader's challenge is to get them to show up to the meetings and make them feel that it is not a waste of their precious time.

Meetings require a quorum, a certain percentage of the listed members who can vote, to be present for business to be conducted, so it is very important to find ways to get people to attend. You may choose to use the carrot-and-stick approach. The stick strategy might require attendance at the meetings with a consequence for nonattendance. It might be that if senators miss two meetings in a term, the funding available to their student group would be frozen for a month or until the next meeting they attend. This method requires attendance to be kept which, in the absence of an electronic tracking system, can be tedious especially for large meetings. More important are the carrots that reward senators for attending the meetings. There are several carrots that can be used, the most essential of which is food. If feasible, you should try to begin every senate meeting with food, either pizza or a sampling of the variety of ethnic fare that is readily available around your school. A second carrot might be to hold a prize drawing for $10 vouchers to your school bookstore. Placing the vouchers at a low dollar amount enables you to give out several at each meeting, which increases the chances of winning. You may want to have a simple prize drawing or a quiz with the first correct answer to each question getting a prize. Giving senator, organization, and committee of the month awards to reward members for noteworthy accomplishments and work encourages them and recognizes the top performing individuals in front of their peers. However, to be realistic, students are pretty smart and while they may have to show up to receive their funding, they are not going to feel the meeting worthwhile simply because they get fed and have the chance to win a prize. The meetings have to be relevant, and this is where the key to a successful organization lies. In student government, there are few things more relevant than inviting administrators to address the students in a formal setting. The more you can facilitate these exchanges, the more relevant the perception of your meetings to both the students and the administration.

While a school administrator may be able to ignore the concerns or complaints of one or two students, the collective voice of elected representatives is very difficult to ignore and could even be potentially unwise. The more often you can put the administration in touch with the students the more likely you are to be successful in your advocacy, provided of course, your advocacy is representative of the collective voice. If possible, the first item on the senate meeting agenda under "New Business" should be a presentation from a school official, a higher-up in the administration with whom you are working closely or someone in a new position at the school. The invited administrator could be expected to speak for ten minutes with five or ten minutes of questions from the senators. These presentations tend to be very useful exchanges, and will be appreciated by both the senators and the administrators. It may surprise you how keen administrators will be to have the opportunity to converse with students, and even though your meeting may be scheduled to be held after the working day, they probably won't mind staying late for the opportunity to speak. Some administrators, typically former teaching faculty, will be very comfortable speaking to a smart and diverse group of elected students, while others may find themselves in a somewhat unfamiliar environment.

When you make the effort to bring pertinent administrators before the senate, it brings with it a certain appreciation from the senate. Most senators will appreciate your efforts at advocacy and the opportunity to give them for an audience with an important school official. So often, business between a student leader and a school official is done in closed session or in a small meeting where the senators and other board members are not invited. It becomes easy to overlook the representative component, which is the real reason you are in the meeting at all. It is tempting for this to become a meeting between two people rather than a meeting between the students and the school leadership. While meetings in these settings are necessary and often the only practical way to accomplish advocacy and to follow up on projects and tasks, giving the senators and school officials the opportunity to come face-to-face serves two very important purposes that cannot be underestimated. It not only reassures the senators that their voice is being heard at the highest level and that the student leader is not merely advancing one's own agenda in their absence, but it also reassures the administrator that the words and advocacy of the student leader in those one-on-one meetings are a representation of the collective view. This gives them more confidence to put school resources, and consequently their own name, behind mitigating a particular student concern.

Another important payoff in establishing the opportunity for the senate to meet an administrator is that it adds a certain understanding and encourages attention, when providing updates to the senators. They can put a face to the name, they will recall the conversation or presentation, and they will feel invested and interested in the outcome of the student leader's follow-up meetings. Ambiguity is removed and a transparency is implied which inspires trust in your leadership, and that is essential for a successful organization.

The senate meeting is much more difficult to control than any other meeting you could lead. There are many more people, all of whom represent a subsection of your constituents, and they can be even more experienced than you! However, you can earn their respect by being transparent, permitting them to speak in the meeting, and ensuring that the meeting stays true to the agenda. Allowing senators to speak in a meeting is essential, because they are the ones who vote and on whom you should rely as barometers of the wider constituency. You should decide and agree with the senate on a set of guidelines for speaking at the meetings. You may have, in your bylaws, a flexible meeting structure that is run by the president, or you may choose to have the meeting be run according to Robert's Rules of Order and chaired by a parliamentarian. Usually, the flexible approach results in a quicker meeting, although senators must feel that they have the opportunity to speak.

Generally, the senate is responsible for the allocation of large amounts of money to student groups. When finance requests exceed the amount that can be considered by the board, you are required to bring them before the senate. Your finance committee or officer should prepare a separate sheet for each senator to accompany the agenda with the name of the organization, the amount requested, the fund from which the money was requested, and the justification and breakdown of the request. You might also want to invite an officer or board member of the organization to be present at the meeting to answer specific questions about the finance request, which will usually help the group's cause. If the organization doesn't send a representative, questions will not be answered appropriately and senators may feel they don't have enough information to justify the amount requested or even their vote. The Appendix includes a sample funding request form.

You should also have a place on the agenda for announcements from the senators. This will have the dual effect of keeping the new business section clear and reserved for important presentations, while giving the senators an opportunity to share their accomplishments or programs or ask for input from others at the meeting. Many senators are working hard and will value the opportunity to share their news with the wider community.

Whatever the size of your organization, or the size and nature of the meeting, if you have been thoughtful and deliberate in your preparation, created a meaningful agenda that has been circulated ahead of time with opportunity for input from the members, and if the meeting starts and finishes on time, then you are well on your way to being a successful student leader.

# Chapter 3

## How to Write or Revise the Constitution and Bylaws

### Overview of Constitution and Bylaws

Webster's dictionary defines a constitution as follows:

A. The basic principles and laws of a nation, state, or social group that determine the powers and duties of the government and guarantee certain rights to the people in it.

B. A written instrument embodying the rules of a political or social organization.

That same dictionary defines a bylaw as "a rule adopted by an organization chiefly for the government of its members and the regulation of its affairs."

The constitution and bylaws are the most important documents of your organization. They are the essential foundations, providing stability and longevity, on which the legacy of your organization will be built. The absence of a constitution and bylaws can render an organization essentially lawless and increase the risk of abuse of authority by those in leadership positions. Officers need to know what is expected of them, with the responsibilities of their position clearly communicated in writing. These documents empower an organization and the board with functions and responsibilities and hold the leaders accountable for their actions. In short, these documents serve to establish the legitimacy of a student organization.

In general, every organization's constitution and bylaws are unique and one group's constitution and bylaws will not necessarily be applicable to another. Likewise, the length of these documents will vary depending on the nature and complexity of the organization. The constitution and bylaws of student governments would typically be longer with more details than those of other kinds of student organizations. The constitution and bylaws should reflect what the organization actually does and need to be accurate and complete in order to be effective.

### Writing the Constitution and Bylaws

Your organization can expect to spend a period of weeks or possibly a few months to write the constitution and bylaws. An ideal time to do this is over the summer when the organization does not usually have as much to do. Writing the constitution and bylaws is an iterative process which involves the following ten steps:

1. **Check on requirements.**

   Typically, a constitution would be required by a school for a group to be formally recognized, and bylaws may be required for a chapter of a national organization. Before you start the process of writing, you should check to see if your school has a suggested layout or certain requirements for the document. In the case of a student chapter, there may be a required format with designated content to include from your national organization. There may even be examples of such documents that you should seek ahead of time.

2. **Determine who will be responsible.**

   The entire process could be managed by a designated committee or officers approved by your board. As a leader, you could either assume responsibility or delegate the task to a committee, such as a judiciary committee. Some organizations prefer to have members approve changes to their constitution and bylaws; however, having too many people involved can make reaching an agreement even harder. Amendments to improve the organization could be delayed due to problems with getting support from a majority of all members.

3. **Brainstorm for ideas.**

   In order to generate ideas for the various sections to be covered in the constitution and bylaws, your team should think about all of the possible words to describe what defines your organization and how your group is to be run. The Appendix includes a sample constitution for a student organization.

4. **Organize the ideas into an outline.**

   Developing a structure and standard for your document will be important. Your organization's documents need to follow all requirements for recognition and chartering by your school and national chapter.

5. **Write out the documents.**

   The quality and the clarity of these documents are very important and will reflect upon your organization. There must be no spelling and grammatical errors (i.e., syntactically correct), and make sure that the writing reflects the intended meaning (i.e., semantically correct). You should try to avoid gender specific wording in the constitution and bylaws by not using pronouns such as he, she, his, her, himself, and herself. Instead, try constructing sentences using the plural forms to avoid using these pronouns. Remember to check the spelling and grammar for all of your documents with a spelling and grammar checker, before e-mailing and submitting them to anyone else for review.

6. **Review with others.**

   Typically, this would require a series of meetings with reviews to find and correct problems, thereby resolving any ambiguities based on feedback from other board members. There could be misleading or vague wording, imbalance of responsibilities, or outdated statements that warrant revision. If possible, have your organization's advisor review these documents for feedback.

7. **Modify to improve.**

   When changes to these draft documents are necessary, you should consider the comments submitted by all those you invited to review the documents. The changes should then be made, and the final draft should be sent to those who reviewed the original document. Your organization's advisor can help in determining whether your proposed changes will actually resolve the issues prior to getting the formal approvals.

8. **Get necessary approvals.**

   Typically, the board and/or senate (in a student government) would need to approve the documents by a majority vote. This democratic approach ensures that the integrity of the organization and the process is preserved.

9. **Submit the documents.**

   Once your constitution and bylaws are finally approved, they should be submitted to your school as part of the formal recognition process. In the case of a chapter of a national organization, you would be expected to send them to that organization for approval of charter status based on your submission.

10. **Publish on your Web site.**

    The constitution and bylaws should be posted on your organization's Web site in HTML and/or PDF formats. Then board, senate, committee, and any other members can read them and, consequently, your organization will appear transparent with a greater level of accountability placed upon the leadership.

## Content of a Constitution

A constitution defines the formation, functions, and representation of the organization and board. There are a number of different articles and sections to include in your organization's constitution, exemplified as follows:

## I. Organization

### A. Name of organization and acronym

The full name of the organization is to be spelled out here. An acronym representing an abbreviation of the organization's name should be mentioned here if applicable. Thereafter, the acronym can be used in place of the organization's name throughout the remainder of this document.

### B. Purpose, Mission, or Objective

The purpose, mission, or objective statement of your organization should reflect the prevailing reason for your group's existence. Getting input from your board members is crucial in forming your organization's mission that is to be spelled out in the constitution.

### C. Membership and Representation

Membership can be divided into voting members and non-voting members, the latter of which may represent affiliated members such as alumni members of your organization. While alumni would not be allowed to serve on the board, they could participate in certain activities and serve on a committee such as an advisory or alumni relations committee to help the organization. For larger student organizations or student governments, representatives from different groups of constituents would typically be defined to form a senate. There could be senators from each school, college, department, or program with the number of representatives proportional to the number of student members in each group.

## II. Board Members

### A. Positions

The size and structure of your organization will determine the number, definition, and responsibilities of positions on the board. The possible titles for positions include President, Vice President, Chair (often applied to a leader of a committee), Coordinator, and Director.

#### i. Duties and responsibilities

The workload should be distributed as evenly as possible, notwithstanding the obvious inequitable responsibilities that accompany certain positions, such as president. The goal, in choosing board positions and assigning responsibilities, is to have consistently high expectations from all members with each member assigned a comparable workload. An imbalance in a role would render any overloaded position less desirable and consequently hard to fill or keep filled.

#### ii. Vacancies

You will need to define the procedures to be followed in the event that an unexpected vacancy is created during the term. Procedures for a special election might be necessary. Alternatively, an executive vice president could assume an officer's work until the position is filled, or a lower ranking board member may be promoted to a higher position for the remainder of the term.

### III. Eligibility, Terms, and Removal

The eligibility for holding a position should be established and stated here. Terms of office should be spelled out for the positions that should last for one academic year. Some organizations even establish term limits. The grounds for removal from office need to be clearly established and communicated.

### IV. Amendments

Your constitution and bylaws need to include a description of how they may be changed. Generally, constitutions are not as easy to amend as bylaws. Bylaws can be typically revised during the academic year, whereas the constitution can usually only be amended once at the end of the year. Any amendments can be appended to the constitution or bylaws for majority approval and inclusion in the following year's updated documents.

### V. Affiliations

There may be additional articles with sections that pertain to your group's affiliation with your school and/or a national organization. You will need to check for such required content.

## Content of the Bylaws

Bylaws typically define the specification for how the organization is to be operated and run, in addition to what actions should or should not be condoned. For bylaws, the following could be defined:

- **Committees and Committee Chairs**

  If not mentioned in the constitution, your organization can separately define committees and the corresponding chairs. Committees can be composed of board members, senators, and general members. Examples of committees include election, judiciary, and programming/activities. Ad hoc committees can be established for special purposes and are usually time limited to determine whether they should become standing committees or merely exist until the issue has been resolved.

- **Procedures and Protocols**

  The procedures for how your organization conducts elections could be detailed in this section. The protocols for how your organization conducts general and/or senate meetings may be included here, for example, whether Robert's Rules of Order are followed or not.

- **Rules and Regulations**

  Your organization may need to establish rules affecting campaigning including contributions and conflicts of interest. This is particularly common in student governments with elected positions by popular vote of the membership. Student governments may institute a judiciary committee to handle violations and removals from office.

- **Policies**

  Your policies should reflect school policies and, therefore, all rules and regulations of your school should be fully understood. In your organization, there must never be any discrimination on the basis of age, gender, race, ethnicity, nationality, creed, disability, and any other characteristics, as dictated by your school policies. Nor should you allow hazing or initiation rites or serve alcohol which will contravene school policy and increase liability. Written policies in your organization's bylaws also serve to protect your group from possible abuse by members.

- **Codes of Conduct**

  The maintenance of ethical standards is crucial for protecting your organization's operation and public image. People do not want to join a scandalous organization, and members are likely to leave the group for another one. Your organization's bylaws can help in providing guidance for conduct.

There may be other sections included in the bylaws as dictated by your school or chapter. In general, the bylaws should be as detailed as necessary and flexible enough to adapt to changing conditions. The Appendix includes a sample set of bylaws for a student organization.

## Enforcement of the Constitution and Bylaws

Enforcement of the constitution and bylaws can either be done by a judiciary committee, typically established for student governments, or by the president in conjunction with the board. You, as a leader, need to set an example by adhering to the constitution and bylaws and making sure that your board abides by them as well. The constitution and bylaws are meaningless unless your leadership follows them. All members must be familiar with the constitution and bylaws, and not knowing them is no excuse for violating them. Board members need to read them before assuming their duties, and reviewing and discussing them at one of your first board meetings should be a priority.

Violators of the constitution and bylaws should be subject to removal from office. Violations could lead to temporary loss of official recognition by your school, or subject your organization to a suspension or probationary period. Board members could resign and members may leave an organization that is faced with disgrace leading to the demise of the group altogether. Violations of the constitution or bylaws by board members should be made known to the regulating body or committee, and a full investigation should be conducted. The establishment of an ethics committee can help with enforcement, and alumni board members can help keep an unbiased perspective to assist in maintaining ethical standards for an organization.

## Revising the Constitution and Bylaws

The membership of your organization may add amendments to the constitution and bylaws at the appointed times. These documents need to be tailored to meet the composition and design of your organization and may need to be updated and refined to reflect changing needs and circumstances facing your group. Changing the constitution or bylaws to lower the standards with poor judgment can have detrimental effects on a student organization. The process of revision is simplified in five steps depicted in Figure 3.

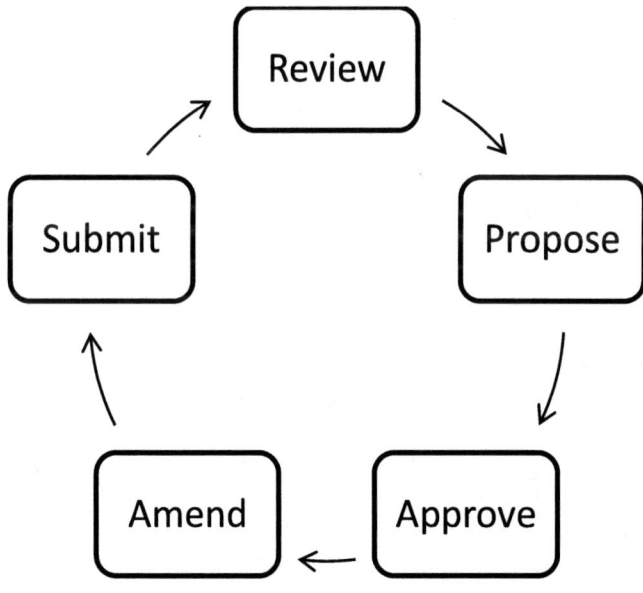

**Figure 3: Revision Cycle**

1. **Review**
   You and your board/committee members should examine and evaluate the documents for ambiguities, deficiencies, errors, inconsistencies, and

omissions. You may also get feedback from former or outgoing officers regarding any specific positions and problems they had with such documents.

2. **Propose**

   Once problems have been identified, you and your board/committee members should propose amendments to correct or clarify any inadequacies.

3. **Approve**

   Any amendments with the exact wording must then be approved by a majority vote of the board, committee, and/or senate in a formal meeting.

4. **Amend**

   Once the document is revised to reflect approved changes, the amendments may be appended to the documents.

5. **Submit**

   The documents should then be submitted to your school to fully incorporate the approved changes. The resulting document should be posted in HTML and/or PDF format on your organization's Web site.

This cycle of revision of the constitution and bylaws should be repeated on an annual basis.

## Epitome

You shouldn't expect the constitution and bylaws to be perfect at the first writing. Much will be learned over time and experience will be the best test and guide for improving these documents. Based on feedback from your predecessors and your own experiences, these documents will be expected to be continually revised in order to improve your organization. There may be gray areas not covered explicitly in your bylaws. In such cases, members and leaders need to follow the spirit of the bylaws, rather than trying to excuse ethically disputable choices simply because the bylaws didn't specifically address the situation. While some may feel that such documents create bureaucracy, these documents will establish the legitimacy and legacy of a democratic student organization.

# Chapter 4

## How to Manage Budgeting, Financing, and Purchasing

### Why Pay a Membership or Programming Fee?

Students are genuinely concerned about the quality of life while gaining their education. The school administration does not have the time or resources to listen to every concern from each student. Therefore, in the interests of an effective and efficient response to the needs of students, an elected student government or elected officers of a student organization are the entities that formally represent students' needs. This is the only way that student programming and advocacy can realistically be addressed to improve the standard of student life on campus. Student government and organizations will need a budget in order to operate effectively. For obvious reasons, they are best funded by students. It is likely, though, that your powers of raising and spending money must fall within school policy, and any variation from these tight rules has the potential to land you and your organization in serious trouble. Your budget will probably be financed by a programming fee, paid by each student to the school, which is funneled to the student organization for disbursement within strict school guidelines.

Most likely, you will have been elected to your position as a student leader due to your successful campaign that promised to address the needs of students. As you prepare for your year in office, it is essential to project the financial resources necessary to meet your election promises. In institutions with well established student organizations and governments, there will probably be limits on how much the student programming fee can be raised each year, either tied in with the rate of inflation or the rate of tuition increase. Accordingly, any measurable increase or decrease in revenue will depend upon student enrollment. The best that you can do is set the programming fee, estimate the enrollment, and allocate the budget on a balance sheet that will change depending upon how close your estimation was to the actual enrollment. Many students pay their own way through school, some live off campus, and most are in school for the academics rather than the student life experience. Therefore, the programming and advocacy preferences will vary for students in different situations and stages of life. Nevertheless, as far as most students are concerned, things could always be better. Campus safety, library holdings, housing, career services, community service, and social programs need money in order to be effective.

Student government exists to ensure that students have the best possible experience on campus through advocacy and programming. From a programming perspective, this means outreach to all students through organizing a variety of interesting events to address programming needs of a very diverse population. When it comes to student government money, responsible disbursement also means devolving responsibility to student organizations who more effectively address certain sections of the student body. From the students' perspective, their main affiliation tends to be with their academic unit, and they may also choose to align themselves with a student interest group. Thus, there is the expectation that their programming fee be distributed to their academic student organization and to the student interest group with which they are aligned. There are also students whose needs may not be met by school-wide programming or programming within their affiliated student organizations. These students will expect some central programming from their student government. The school administration, however, tends to consider that students are admitted primarily to the school and they become citizens of the school and members of the school family. As such, they are able to take advantage of the many lectures, concerts, and special events organized by the school for the pleasure of the whole school community. Therefore, there may be the expectation from the school administration that some of the students' programming fee, collected by the student government, should support school-wide programming.

The position of being a leader with a budget in student government is a finely balanced one, being part of the greater school community, representing the general constituency, and being responsible for the numerous student groups that are under the auspices of student government. As a student leader, you will be expected to satisfy the expectations of the students by providing money to their student organizations, school administration by contributing towards school-wide programming, and school population by advocating and programming for them.

## Setting the Budget

A student government will require a relatively large budget from which other student groups will request much smaller amounts of money for their operational budget. Student government will be accountable to the school administration, while student groups will be accountable to the student government. As a student leader, you will likely be required to give an annual account of your fiscal activities. Therefore, it is imperative that you have a solid tracking system for your money and that you know how you acquire funds at the beginning of the academic year, how your organization will spend that money, and how you will account for it.

Budgets may range from the hundreds of dollars in the case of student groups to hundreds of thousands of dollars in the case of student governments. The sources of funding depend on the school and organization and possible funding sources for student groups include the following: Budget allocated through the school, the student governing organization, the department, sponsorship from various campus services (e.g., campus bookstore, housing, food, and transportation), membership fees, and outside sponsors.

It goes without saying that students know best what they need. If students are willing to pay a small programming fee each year for an improvement in quality of life, they are more likely to want that money disbursed by their peers rather than by the administration. Setting a budget for student government will have to be done thoughtfully based upon providing a real service for the fee. It is unlikely that students will have any choice to opt out of paying the programming fee; therefore, it is incumbent upon the student government to set the fee appropriately. Setting the programming fee and budget of a student government will depend upon what the perceived need is (what is provided already and what is desired), the cost of student government (running the office and paying staff), and the amount that students will be willing to pay. While it is possible to raise the programming fee, such raises will occur prior to student enrollment, so there can be no boosting of the coffers mid-way through a year of low enrollment. Such increases in the programming fee will have to occur in the following year. Whether you are starting a new group or inheriting the reins of an established organization, the budgetary challenges are similar.

## Above-the-line Income and Expenses

The budget categories and accounts will probably have been established from the very beginning of the organization, with approval from the senate and agreement from the school administration. Certain above-the-line expenses will have been agreed upon, and these categories will contain allocations based on a percentage of the income or on a fixed amount that is independent of the income. Above-the-line expenses will have to be *paid* first, and the remaining amount is used to drive the rest of the budget.

For the purposes of illustration, let us imagine a school with 5,000 students and a budget shown in the table and charts at the end of this chapter. In the example given here, the student government raises its money solely from the enrolled student population. In reality, there may be some rollover from the previous year where all of the money was not spent or, in extreme cases of fortuity, there may be some money from an endowment. However, for the purposes of this illustration, the funds will be assumed to come from the student population. Thus, by charging each of the 5,000 students $50 per year, the annual budget for the student government in this example is $250,000. In this example, there are several above-the-line expense items that will either be tied to the revenue or will be fixed costs regardless of the revenue. For example, if your student government merits the hiring of full or part-time employees, their salary will be based on a fixed amount as per the school pay scale including benefits and will be independent of the revenue generated by student enrollment and the programming fee. The employees will need to be paid the same amount regardless of how many students are enrolled. An additional fixed cost will be the tuition remission for the elected board officers, if such a provision is made. This cost will be fixed at the rate of tuition and will vary depending on the number of elected officers and upon the number of units of remitted tuition per officer, which may vary depending on the work expectation. However, if your student government allocates some money to the school for school-wide programming, that allocation will probably be a percentage of the programming fee. Since programming for students can only be provided to the number of students who are enrolled, it makes sense that a proportion of the income, rather than a fixed amount, would drive this allocation. In this example, there is an agreement to allocate the school administration 8% of the total revenue for school-wide programming. In the current example, the difference between the above-the-line revenue and expenses is $192,000 ($250,000 - $58,000), and from this amount the rest of the budget can be created.

## Expenditures

The remainder of the budget will have accounts that have also been established by a vote from the senate, and the amount in each category or account will be determined as either a percentage or a fixed amount of the funds available after the above-the-line expenses. For example, it may be the decision of the senate that academic programming should be fixed at a certain amount that does not vary with student enrollment, but social programming might vary with enrollment. It might conceivably be that the Discretionary or Volunteer accounts are fixed amounts up to a certain enrollment, above which they begin to represent the extra enrollment by having a percentage of the income from the additional students allocated to those accounts. However the budget is apportioned and whatever categories are chosen, there will need to be some contingency amount built into the budget in case the student enrollment is less than anticipated.

While some larger organizations may have more than enough money, depending upon their programming goals, some smaller groups may have to deal with not having enough money to meet their goals. Dealing with under-funded organizations can be a real challenge and while fundraising, sponsorship, and joint programming with other groups may be possible, minimization of expenditures greatly helps.

## The Cost of Student Government

A certain amount will be required for the effective running of the student government itself. From this money, the office expenses, staff salaries, and student pay or tuition remission will be drawn, in addition to the programming that you, as the leader, have outlined in your vision for the year. Student governments will need to determine whether or not to compensate their officers and if so, whether compensation is in the form of tuition remission, stipends, or other benefits. Such decisions will probably be influenced by the size of the student body and the rate being paid for other on-campus or local jobs. Generally, the board is composed of officers with specific responsibilities, and most of them would have a financial allocation to accomplish their goals and fulfill their election promises. For example, the officer responsible for academic programming will need money to host academic events for all students to attend, possibly to pay an honorarium and pay for food and/or room rental.

Student government, unlike most student organizations, is an administratively heavy unit that requires a large amount of money to sustain. Hopefully, the students who pay the programming fee will feel that the expense required to keep the student government functioning will be worth it. If there is an office, there may need to be an office assistant. For some of the bigger academic institutions, this will be in the form of a full-time employee, whose salary will be paid from the student programming fee. This person will also need an administrative account to operate the office. Depending on the number of elected student officers, there will need to be computers, phone lines, chairs, desk space, storage, and supplies. While all officers will be required to keep office hours, they can be staggered to share space and resources thus cutting down on those costs. You will notice that the cost of running the student government in the given example is $40,000 including staff salary ($30,000), officer tuition remission ($5,000), and the administrative budget ($5,000) for maintaining the office. This figure will vary depending on the size of the student population, the need for full- or part-time staff, and the cost of remitting tuition.

## Board Programming

The names of the accounts should describe their intended use. In the example presented here, there are accounts for the board of officers to use for the purpose of their elected role, such as Administrative, Academic Programming, Community Service, Recruitment, Public Relations, Social Programming, and Committee Support. While these accounts are for the use of the officers, the amounts will have been previously agreed by the senate that served the previous year. In the example given, the student government board is responsible for spending 14% of the budget, and with the exception of the administrative account used to run the office, $30,000 ($35,000 - $5000) is used for officer and committee programming for the school student population.

As stated earlier, all money must be spent in accordance with the school guidelines. One such policy is the prohibition on buying alcohol, even when all the students attending the event are over 21 years old. It is also prohibitive to misappropriate school money by spending on oneself, and there should be a huge emphasis on ethical and appropriate use of student funds. As a student leader, you will be held accountable for the spending of your officers, and you should hold them to the highest levels of fiscal integrity.

## Senate Programming

The majority of the budget, as it should be, is administered by the senate for use by officially recognized student organizations of the school. This money is apportioned in accounts that will, by virtue of the amounts allocated to each, drive the programming of the student body. In the given example, there are four accounts: the Interdisciplinary Programming fund is available for programming between two academically or socially disparate groups; the Volunteer Programming fund is for community service themed events; the Discretionary fund is for any event not covered by the previous two funds and serves as a catch-all and hence is the largest fund available; and the Conference Travel fund is used to support students who may need to attend an academic conference to present a research paper. Within each fund, there may be a maximum amount that can be available for any one group or event, set at the discretion of the senate at the time the bylaws are being revised. For example, it may be that any one student may only receive a maximum of $300 from the Conference Travel fund per year. It may also be that there is a $1,000 limit on each event funded through any of the other three accounts. This helps spread the money around to the various student groups and helps prevent running out of money before the end of the academic year.

In the given example, the largest budget allocation, $155,000 or 62% of $250,000 (the total budget) is reserved for senate programming. Of this, almost 68% or $105,000 is set aside as a pre-allocation to the student organizations that are tied to the programs in which students are enrolled. While this is technically administered by the student government, it is an automatic allocation to any officially recognized academic student organization with a constitution and officers. This means that while the student group needs to request and justify the expenditure of its funds, the pre-allocation means that the organization does not need a vote from either the board or senate in order to receive the funds. This allocated amount is based on enrollment in the program, and with this model the students know that approximately 42% of their $50 programming fee (42% of $250,000 = $105,000) is allocated directly to their home department's student organization for events specific to them.

Many academic units tend to have well-structured student organizations that represent the needs of their particular students. For some big and diverse academic units, there may be an umbrella organization with subdivisions that form along the more specific disciplines. For instance, there may be an umbrella student organization for the school, while also some smaller groups for students of a department, etc. Large programs with hundreds of students will receive a large allocation from the student programming fee, permitting a broad array of social and academic programs that appeal to a diverse student body (something for everyone). However, small programs with few students will receive a small amount of money, and this amount may only be enough for programming one pizza party or other event per term.

One of the main roles of the student government is to ensure that as many academic units have student groups that have been officially recognized by the school administration, in order to receive their 42% allocation. It may be the case that in small departments, there is no functioning student organization. In the given example, a department with ten students would be entitled to $210 for their own programming. There will probably be a school deadline by which all student groups must be registered for recognition and after that date, any unclaimed money will roll into a contingency fund and, if the senate agrees, be reallocated into one of the main accounts for general programming.

## Adjustments to the Budget

Final enrollment numbers are often not available until a few weeks into the term, so your initial budget must be projected based on an estimate of student numbers. Usually, after the third week of classes or so, the school enrollment report is generated and accurate numbers of students enrolled in various majors can be plugged into the budget. If there are a greater number of students paying the programming fee, then this increased revenue can be distributed to the other accounts administered by the board or the senate, with approval from the senate. It is up to the finance committee to present a recommendation to the senate based on their perceived need and the greater opportunities for programming that may become available with more income. Conversely, if there is a decrease in enrollment, it is hoped that the contingency will cover it. In the given example, the contingency allows for a drop in enrollment of 1.2%, which is small, though it is important to know that academic institutions have very tight control of their admits, and a 1 or 2% drop would be unlikely unless it was part of the school enrollment strategy. However, in the event that the contingency does not cover a decrease in enrollment, the senate would then have to agree where the budget deficit was going to be met, again upon hearing a presentation from the finance committee.

As mentioned earlier, you cannot increase the programming fee upon suddenly discovering that you have a deficit. Budget setting must be agreed by the senate annually, usually at the end of the year in preparation for the following year. At that time, all budget items are up for discussion; once a budget has been approved by the senate, it must be ratified by the school administration. However, there is some flexibility within the agreed budget to move money between accounts if required. For example, it is likely that some accounts will be exhausted prior to the end of the academic year, while others will be underutilized. In such a scenario, the finance officer may make a presentation to the senate arguing that, for example, since the Volunteer Programming account is almost depleted while the Interdisciplinary Programming account is unlikely to be used up, a transfer of funds is recommended to further support the popular volunteer programming. This would also need to be approved by a majority vote of the senate.

It may also be that the programming fee is collected each term rather than once per year, and that would mean that each student would pay a certain amount of money per year. This slightly complicates the budget since there will be a lag in calculating the total budget available. It may mean that not all of the organizational allocation can be spent in the first term, because it will be unlikely that an advance will be available. There is also the possibility that enrollment in each term will be different due to attrition, graduation, or increased enrollment. All these issues must be considered in creating and administering a budget. In Table 4, a budget imbalance of $2000 is a surplus instituted as a precautionary measure to account for a possible budget shortfall, leading to a deficit with budget cuts to balance the budget.

## Requesting Money

As a student leader with a budget, you need to have an uncomplicated and effective strategy for permitting students to request money and for the board or senate to approve the allocation of the funds. For student governments, computerized submission of funding via Web site forms would greatly improve efficiency of processing funding requests from student groups.

The mechanism by which students request funding will be in either paper or electronic format to be reviewed by the finance officer and the finance committee. There should be some criteria for a funding request in order to help those voting on the proposal to make a decision. Your board should establish evaluation criteria for selection, making a successful proposal, and advise other organizations on what makes a successful budget request including proper cost estimation. The first screening point will be whether the student group is officially registered with the school. A student group that is not officially recognized by the school cannot usually receive school funds. Once the organization's eligibility has been determined, it is necessary to get information about the event, such as the date, time, event title, description, people invited to attend and, more specifically, estimated number of students that will attend. It is important to remember that since the funds have been paid by students, they should be spent on students. Thus, a funding request from a student group that may comprise both students and non-students, but is predominantly non-students, may expect to receive funding in proportion to the number of students involved, no matter how large the overall attendance or how much money is needed.

## Approving Finance Requests

For money that is available to any student group, disbursement of the funds must be approved by a majority vote of the board or senate, probably depending upon the amount requested. These requests tend to take up a lot of time, since many student groups will submit funding requests. In order to help mitigate the time, the finance officer and finance committee should provide an initial review and make recommendations to the voting body. It may be that the finance committee recommends an amount of $250, while the student group has applied for $300. The vote therefore will be against the two amounts, unless alternate amounts are suggested from the voting members.

It may be more efficient to differentiate the approval process for requests over a certain amount. Typically, smaller amounts need to be approved only by the board, whereas the larger amounts need to be approved by the full senate. The implications of these processes mean that since the board is more likely to meet more frequently than the senate, smaller requests will receive approval more quickly than larger ones. This might drive the type of programming among the student body, though a visionary student organization will have the foresight to plan well ahead and request larger amounts months in advance. Since funding requests need to be approved by a majority vote, there will typically be questions that officers will have prior to voting. It is a useful strategy for the requesting student organization to be present at the meeting to answer these questions. There will also need to be a time for calling for alternate funding amounts from the officers or senate that will also need to be voted on. The alternate amounts will probably be proposed as a result of the answer to the officers' questions by the representative of the requesting organization. It is unlikely that the alternate amount will be greater than the amount requested, and sometimes the alternate amount proposed will be zero. The committee will vote on the amounts set before them, and there will be a run-off between the two amounts that received the most votes. Finally, the committee will have a majority vote, and that vote needs to be recorded in the minutes of the meeting. The finance committee chair would then be responsible for contacting the student organization and informing them of the outcome.

For those student organizations that are not student governments, the process of finance requests may be simplified. Members should present a budget proposal in writing detailing the type of event, purpose, cost including detailed expenses (food, supplies, prizes, etc.), and expected participation with the percentage of members from your organization. The proposal should be submitted in writing or via e-mail to be sent out to all board members who would vote on the request.

## Disbursing Funds

There are some financial terms that you will likely encounter:
1. Purchase orders (to purchase items from outside your school)
2. Requisitions (to make purchases within your school)
3. Vendors (companies or providers approved to do business with your school)
4. Reimbursement (to pay back for expenses)

Given the sensitivity to fiscal accountability, it will be in the best interests of a student government to administer the funding within strict guidelines. This can take time, but given that audits from the school administration may occur frequently, and given that your role is to remain in satisfactory standing with the school administration, it is time well spent. If, as in this example, each student organization is entitled to a pre-allocation of funds, the mechanism for requesting these funds can be fairly easy. If your student government has a finance officer or committee, they should be able to approve such requests as long as the request identifies how the money will be spent, and that the spending of that money is within the school policies. It is important to require receipts to be submitted after each funding allocation and before the next one, in order to reconcile the request with the actual expenses. The finance officer will be responsible for filling out paperwork authorizing the school's financial services office to cut a check for a particular student group or to arrange for an internal requisition, depending on whether the services are from within or outside the school.

Money that goes directly to the school's administration for school-wide programming will be a contribution to a much larger budget, and such funds are most likely transferred without the need for a funding request. In this case, the school, being its own auditor, will not be required to provide you with receipts for the spending of this pre-allocation.

## Buying

Academic institutions are usually very concerned about where their money is spent, even the relatively small amount of programming money that is paid by the students to the student government. This concern has resulted in a vetting process that renders a decision on whether a non-school vendor can do business with the school. In order to be approved by the school, vendors must be willing to share some important information, including their taxpayer ID number with the school for the purposes of being paid. Once vendors are approved, whether they are caterers, keychain manufacturers, or travel companies, dealing with them is relatively easy and is usually a matter of filing a form with all relevant information. School payment to vendors is well documented and most likely occurs from the financial services office. Receipts are provided for the services rendered, and records should be kept for the purposes of an audit. As a student leader, it is very important for you to ethically and accurately manage the finances of your organization and to disburse funds transparently within your school guidelines. It is also important for you to have an intuitive and non-cumbersome requesting process for student organizations and that regular budget updates are provided to the board and senate. You will earn respect quickly if you can manage money ethically and responsibly, and school administrators are more likely to be predisposed towards working on issues of advocacy with a student leader who can be trusted with money.

The following table is a sample budget detailing the sources of revenue, expenses, and net budget balance for an academic year from one calendar year to the next.

## Table 4: Sample budget for Student Government

| Academic Year | | 201x to 201x+1 |
|---|---|---|
| Revenue | | |
| Total Estimated Students | | 5,000 |
| Total Fees Collected | $ | 50.00 |
| **Total Amount Collected** | **$** | **250,000.00** |
| Expenses | | |
| Contingency | $ | (3,000.00) |
| Staff Salaries | $ | (30,000.00) |
| Tuition Remission | $ | (5,000.00) |
| School-wide Program Funding | $ | (20,000.00) |
| **Above-the-line items** | **$** | **(58,000.00)** |
| Accounts | | |
| Administrative | $ | 5,000.00 |
| Academic Programming | $ | 10,000.00 |
| Community Service | $ | 2,000.00 |
| Recruitment | $ | 1,000.00 |
| Public Relations | $ | 5,000.00 |
| Social Programming | $ | 10,000.00 |
| Committee Support | $ | 2,000.00 |
| *Board Programming* | *$* | *35,000.00* |
| Conference Travel | $ | 10,000.00 |
| Discretionary | $ | 20,000.00 |
| Interdisciplinary Programming | $ | 10,000.00 |
| Volunteer | $ | 10,000.00 |
| Student Organization Funding | $ | 105,000.00 |
| *Senate Programming* | *$* | *155,000.00* |
| **Accounts Subtotal** | **$** | **190,000.00** |
| *Budget Imbalance* | *$* | *2,000.00* |

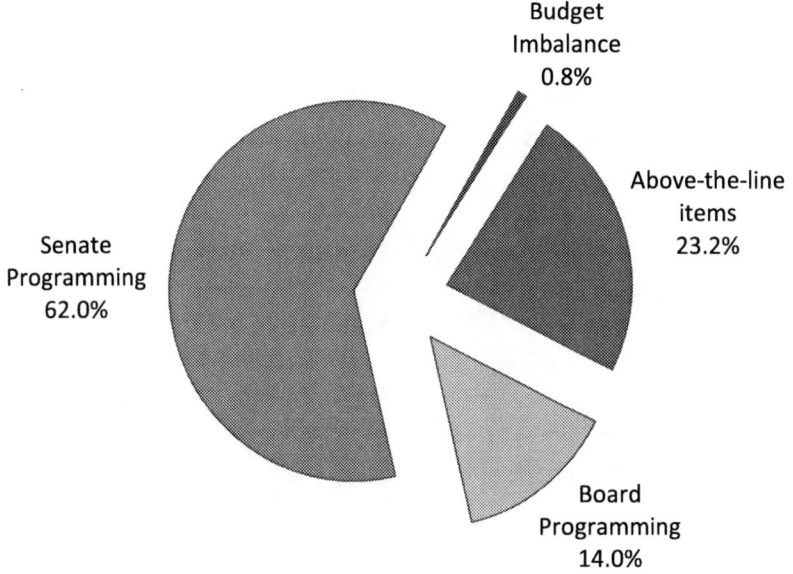

**Figure 4-1: Funding Distribution for Student Government Budget**

The following figures represent each slice of the pie chart in Figure 4-1, except for the Budget Imbalance.

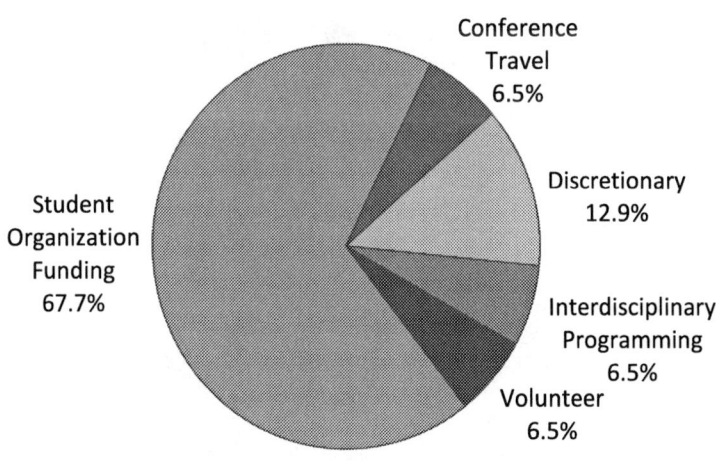

**Figure 4-2: Senate Programming Funding Distribution**

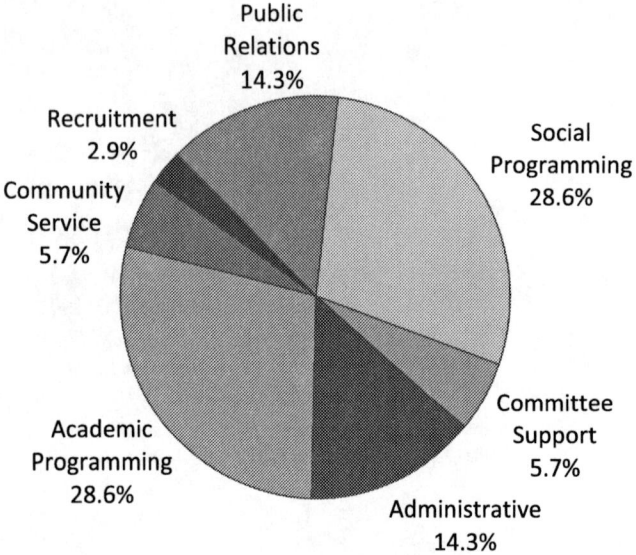

**Figure 4-3: Board Programming Funding Distribution**

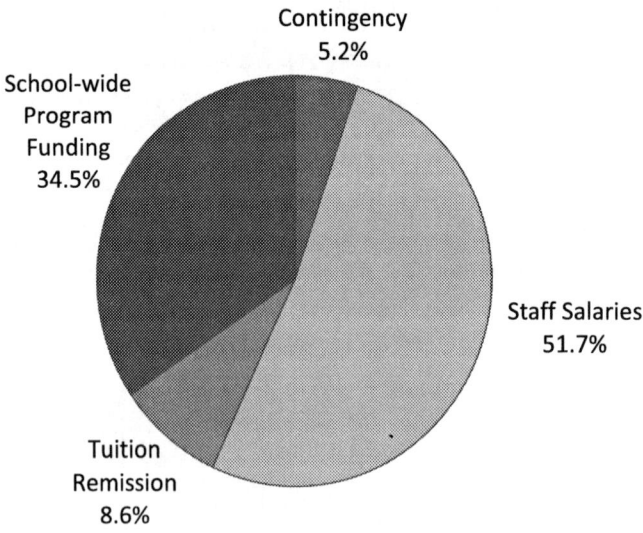

**Figure 4-4: Above-the-line Items Funding Distribution**

# Chapter 5

# How to Promote and Publicize an Organization

## Why Promote and Publicize?

No matter how well attended your events have been in a given term or year, or no matter how successful your prior advocacy, each year, there will be a new influx of students who will have never heard of your organization. This means that you will always have to engage in a cycle of publicity and promotion in order to recruit new members, proclaim your successes, and advertise your upcoming activities to your current members. Relentless publicity should be the role of an officer and/or committee with a budget to allow them to succeed and grow your organization. There are several methods of promoting and publicizing your organization, and some of them will be presented here.

## Establishing a Web site and E-mail Accounts

Your organization's Web site will be the primary source of publicity and information about your group and the more professional it is, the better the reflection of your group. On your Web site you can highlight your organization's mission statement, goals, and accomplishments. You have the opportunity to really impress the Web site visitors, not just with the professionalism of your site but with the substance of your organization, and to show why your group is valuable by what you do for your members and for your school. Elaborate and content rich graphics on a Web site may be harder to maintain but can be quite impressive. Make sure that your Web pages load well on mobile devices and slower speed connections to the Internet, such as a dial-up connection, by setting the default view to HTML with any Flash/Silverlight content optional on your Web site. Keeping an accurate and up-to-date Web site is very important, and there should be no misspellings or grammatical errors.

Typically, schools provide network accounts to officially recognized organizations at no cost, so your group should establish an account for e-mail and a Web site that bears the name of your organization. A common Web site address would be www.yourschool.edu/your_org. Your school will probably assign a Web site address in line with established naming policies. If network services are not provided by your school, an alternative approach would be to establish your own ".org" Web site, although this would involve a cost. A site name for a ".org" could be www.acronym-of-your-school_acronym-of-your-organization.org. You may use a delimiter (period, dash, and underscore) between the acronyms as in any e-mail address. With Internet Information Services (Windows Server) or Apache (Linux/Unix) installed on your own computer you could build your own Web server, but this approach may be difficult and expensive, requiring skilled people for set-up, maintenance, and support. However, one advantage with this approach is that you can create your own e-mail accounts from the server for board members and committee chairs which some institutions are unable or unwilling to do. A common e-mail address is ACRONYM@yourschool.edu, where the acronym is an initialism of your organization's name.

You should test your Web site within multiple versions of operating systems including Windows (PC), Macintosh OS X, and Linux/Unix, using different Web browsers such as Internet Explorer, Mozilla Firefox, and Apple Safari. Your site should be easy to read with proper color combinations, contrasts between foreground and background, readable font sizes, and minimal scrolling on pages. Navigation and fully functioning links should all work properly on each page.

You can use your Web site to recruit committee members, announce open positions on your board, and announce other opportunities for members to be involved. You can even have Web links to other sites such as departments, partner student organizations, relevant sites for new students (housing, registration), and links to community activities. You should seek permission from administrators to get your organization's Web site linked from any relevant department or school, in order to help people (particularly new students) find out about your group. Digital photographs of events and members can be added to your organization's Web site as they occur, posting them as thumbnails that can be enlarged when clicked. Answers to frequently asked questions (FAQ) can be posted on your Web site, and you can set up a committee to accumulate and answer these questions. There should also be a prominent link to your organization's Constitution and Bylaws which will help members and visitors understand your group's structure. A chatterbox or blog can be placed on the Web site, however the content is difficult to monitor and control. Unless your group is able to moderate these, there is a risk that people may post erroneous information or rumors that could publicly embarrass your organization.

E-mail addresses of board members, committee chairs, and/or the group are typically found on an organization's Web site. If you need extra accounts for special purposes that your school does not provide, you could take a look at the many free e-mail accounts available to set up. These can be set up for individual officers, committee chairs, committees, etc. Due to the high volume of e-mail that can be sent and received about organizational matters, such additional e-mail accounts are recommended to avoid any problems with capacity constraints. Instead of posting email addresses on a Web site, contact forms may be used to avoid spammers, with submissions forwarded to the appropriate individuals.

## Creating and Distributing Brochures and Flyers

One of the best ways to let people know about your organization is to create a brochure or flyer, and distribute it as widely as possible. Ideally, the brochure or flyer would be ready for distributing to incoming students and posted at orientation events or your first meeting of the new school year. Your promotional literature should succinctly and creatively project the mandate and personality of your organization and should, at a minimum, contain the following information:

- Acronym for organization
- Complete name of organization
- Organization's Web site
- Organization's e-mail address
- Upcoming event information

Given the relative ease of creating flyers on personal computers and the increasing availability of user-friendly software, your brochure will need to be spectacular in every aspect in order to compete with other organizations and earn the respect of potential members as well as the student body at large. You should consider including graphics or photographs from recent events; however, you must be careful not to infringe on any trademarks or copyrights by using unauthorized words, phrases, designs, or photographs. Even logos from your school are typically governed by strict policies regarding use, color, size, and the nature of the content the logo will be effectively endorsing. Again you should make sure that the flyers comply with your school's policies, especially regarding alcohol and potentially offensive images, and your group should not violate school rules by posting on unapproved locations. You may have to get permission to post on a bulletin board. To avoid removal before the time of the event, include a complete date with the month, day, and year on your flyer. One of the biggest problems with posting flyers is overcrowding on the typically small official posting stations. Only one flyer is needed on a single bulletin board, and your group should be mindful of other organizations taking care not to post over another flyer for an event that has not already occurred. Doing so could hurt your group's reputation and generate ill will from other organizations who share the same posting sites. Small flyers can be generated, copied, and distributed by board members in the main campus areas that are frequented by potential members at lunchtime. As the leader of your organization, you will be held responsible for the appropriateness of your publications. Once the literature design and text have been approved by your board, you can seek a printing company or a copying service to duplicate your materials.

A logo can be designed for your student organization, if one does not already exist. The logo should contain the acronym and/or name of your organization and capture the focus of your group. You may also want to include the school to which you belong. Make sure your designs are permissible by your school and do not violate any policies regarding the use of your school name and their logo(s). Logos can be designed using graphical design software such as Adobe Illustrator/Photoshop or Microsoft Expression Design, and it is essential to get help from a member who is skillful in the use of such software. The logo will be added to printed and electronic media (e.g., your group's Web site), t-shirts, and other promotional items, in addition to the letterhead on which you mail your official letters. Banners, table cloths, and flags bearing your logo can all be designed for your student organization to display at your events, and your public relations officer/chair should be responsible for the purchase of such items. Do not underestimate the impact of an effective logo and branding on your organization. If your organization has artistic or creative members who can design logos, you might want to have a competition with a significant prize awarded for the one selected by the board, committee, or senate. The life of the logo will long outlive your time in office and appropriate attention and, if necessary a budget, should be given to its creation.

## Purchasing and Distributing Promotional Items

Promotional items can be a source of great publicity, particularly the fun, unusual, or really useful items. There are many promotional items that can be distributed to members and friends of your organization including baseball caps, business card holders, compasses, flashlights, highlighters, key chains, mugs, pencils, pens, rulers, t-shirts, and whistles. You can get your organization's name, logo, Web site, e-mail address, and other designs printed on these items. Many promotional items are expensive, especially when the cost of adding a logo is considered and your organization will have to carefully budget enough money for these items. Your public relations officer or committee should be charged with exploring a number of possible vendors and getting quotes on the pricing and delivery arrangements in terms of shipping and time to receive, in order to ensure that the best deal is secured. Distributing promotional items to incoming students is a great way of generating awareness, especially if the promotional items are useful or intriguing. Clothing tends to be more expensive and, depending on your organization's budget, should be reserved for a select group such as board members, advisors, staff, senators, or committee chairs/members. You should ensure that proper sizes will be ordered by having recipients sign up in advance with their size preference indicated.

## Tabling

Setting up a table somewhere on campus is a great method for generating visibility to attract members to your organization and distribute promotional items and materials. You can set up a table at an involvement or activities fair that your school may hold annually or at the beginning of each term, or a table may be set up somewhere that is easily visible to a lot of potential members. There may be tabling policies at your school and, in advance, you should check for any restrictions or possible reservations needed.

The table should be staffed around lunchtime (11 am to 2 pm) anytime Monday through Friday with approximately 30 minutes allowed for setting up and taking down. Try to have more than one officer of your organization at the table, so that there are extra people to handle two or more students who may come by at the same time. You can divide up the time slots so that each available officer is stationed at the table for 30-60 minutes. It is important to have enough brochures, flyers, and membership forms to distribute. The goal of tabling should be to make your organization's presence obvious and to get contact information of interested students.

## Speaking at Orientation or Other Events

A great way to let new students know about your organization is to speak at orientation events. This will help in getting students involved in the beginning, given the short stay that many students, especially those in master's degrees or certificate programs, may have in school. Typically, you will need to get permission from the relevant administrators to have your organization represented at the orientation events, and you should only target orientations for students you would draw members from. For instance, a departmental or school organization would target its department or school orientations; however, a student government would target the orientation events for the whole incoming class.

## Creating a Mailing List

A listserv or mailing list can be set up to send out e-mail to members and other students who may have signed up at an orientation, tabling, or other social events. A listserv allows members to sign up and unsubscribe on their own, thus freeing up time spent managing the list. To create a list, your public relations officer/chair could search through the school directory to find members and send the promotional or informational e-mail without disclosing individual addresses by using a listserv, mailing list, Yahoo group, Google group, bcc (blind carbon copy), or lcc (list carbon copy). Mailing lists can be moderated or unrestricted with respect to who has sending privileges. Unrestricted lists may cause people to send unnecessary e-mails, spam, or may even spread viruses. A moderated listserv with sending privileges restricted to board members will control for unsolicited mail and will be appreciated by the members on the list. Even with a moderated listserv, it is important not to send too many e-mails in a week or to send out unauthorized or inaccurate messages (such as incorrect times, venues, statistics, news updates) that will have to be corrected as soon as possible by a subsequent corrective message. Such mistakes are very embarrassing, show a lack of professionalism, and may lead members to unsubscribe.

If your message contains multiple items, as typically found in a newsletter, it is advisable to put a table of contents with links at the top of the e-mail, so that students can easily navigate the message or bypass it altogether if nothing is of interest to them, without having to read through the whole message. The convenience of readers being able to glance at the contents without wasting time reading more than they need to will help retain subscribers. Your audience is also more likely to look at the message instead of ignoring it and potentially missing some important information. A weekly newsletter can be e-mailed to members mentioning upcoming and ongoing events and activities. It is very important to check the contents for spelling and grammatical errors as well as the accuracy of the information before sending it out. Any URLs or e-mail addresses can be included for further information to reduce the size of the newsletter, which is very important since large e-mails (with attachments) can put students' mailboxes over quota and consequently lead them to unsubscribe from your list. Printed newsletters can be expensive, time-consuming, hard to distribute and cannot be updated, while an attractive online newsletter can easily be placed on your organization's Web site and updated if necessary.

## Other Advertising Strategies

Newsgroups can also be set up, although the problem is that students will often not know when a new message will be available and timely information could be missed. Therefore, while newsgroups are effective ways for members to make announcements or to sell things, they are less effective than e-mail announcements for conveying important time-sensitive information.

Yearbook pictures are another way to promote your organization, albeit unlikely that new students would be reached in this manner. Similarly, advertisements in school newspapers can be an effective way of promoting your organization. However, there are usually considerable costs associated with advertising in newspapers and yearbooks, and you should consider the readership numbers and demographics when deciding whether the expense will yield a worthwhile return. Some schools even have radio or television stations offering additional media for advertisement, but your organization should determine carefully how the public relations budget would be best spent beforehand.

If your school has electronic signs at the entrance gates or around campus, you may be able to promote your organization and events through these forms of media. Some departments and schools have their own online calendars where you may be able to advertise your organization and events. Given the limited space on such media, you must make sure that the information about your events is succinct. To help students get further information about the events, you should include your organization's Web site and e-mail address in these forms of advertising if possible.

## Offering Food and Drinks

One of the best ways to promote your organization is to offer food at an event. Your organization will have to decide on the type of food to order, the vendor and the amount to purchase for each event. Your organization should explore different local vendors to find out which ones will give you the best deal, including any special deals for students. There may be a specified list of approved vendors for your school you must order from, or you may have to work with new vendors and get them approved by your school before you can order from them. You should always check the Web site of your local health department to see if a food vendor has any health code violations. Typically pizza and sandwiches are ordered to save costs and simplify food distribution. Remember to include some vegetarian selections and, if possible, estimate the number of vegetarians in your organization to ensure enough food is available for them.

One of the biggest challenges is deciding how much food to order and how much to give for each person. To help with the calculations, there is a useful formula that follows:

$$T = A \times \frac{P}{S}$$

$A$ = (estimated) number of attendees
$P$ = number of pieces
$S$ = number of servings
$T$ = total number of food items or drinks

The $\times$ in the formula represents the multiplication sign. Pieces are the amount each person will receive. Servings apply to food that is divisible.

$S = 1$ if the food item is not divisible. For drinks in cans or small bottles such as soda, $S = 1$. For drinks in bottles that are served in cups, $S$ would be equal to the number of cups per bottle. The assumption is that the food is the same size; otherwise the formula must be applied to each separate size of food. Also, if the food is of different types or flavors, you can apply the formula to every type to come up with how much of each can be given out at the event. For food such as pizza, this formula can be easily applied. In the following example, an event with 100 people attending, with each pizza consisting of 12 slices, and with 3 slices allowed per person, the number of pizzas necessary would be 25 computed as follows:

$$T = 100 \times \frac{3}{12} = 25$$

Similarly, if you have already ordered pizza and you want to know how many slices each person can have who has attended the event, you should count the number of members present and solve for $P$. In the following example, having ordered 25 pizzas cut into 12 slices each, and with 150 people at the event, the number of slices per person would be 2.

$$P = T \times \frac{S}{A} = 25 \times \frac{12}{150} = 2$$

This formula can be applied to party-style sandwiches where the individual servings of a long (6-foot) sandwich have been cut. To be sure that you feed everyone you should determine $A$ by counting the number of attendees before you serve.

For cases where the food has not been pre-cut and you need to make the slices yourself, you would solve for $S$ using the following formula:

$$S = A \times \frac{P}{T}$$

For food, drinks, and supplies, remember to round $T$ to the next whole number, in order to avoid problems with having fractional amounts in your total. For example, if $T > 24$ and $T < 25$, then $T$ becomes 25. You can even use this formula to decide how many plates, cups, napkins, and utensils to order, though you should always have extra amounts of these supplies available.

You should always order the food well in advance of the event. Failure to order food in advance will result in the embarrassing position of having an event at which food was promised, and none was available. When you are having the food delivered, you should make sure that the deliverer does not get lost on your campus, and you should exchange mobile phone numbers with the deliverer to ensure that the delivery goes smoothly. This is very important when dealing with new vendors who may not have been on campus before, or during times when the campus is densely populated, such as at homecoming, where multiple events mean that it would be difficult for the deliverer to find your event amidst all the others occurring at the same time. To avoid any delivery charges, food can be picked up by a reliable board member. Pizza boxes should be kept closed as much as possible during the time that food is being distributed and drinks should be kept in coolers or buckets filled with ice, preferably well in advance of the event so that the drinks will be cold at the time food is served. People handling food should wash their hands before handling food and wear hygiene gloves. Serving utensils should be available for all food to be served (e.g. nuts, chips), and a server should be available for these food stations as well.

The goal in serving food at an event is to encourage attendance, while ensuring that everyone gets fed something first before allowing seconds and thirds to attendees. An officer and several board/committee members should be responsible for the distribution in an orderly fashion, with the amount of food being carefully regulated. Remember that running out of food or drinks can be very embarrassing and could deter people from attending future events. As part of the evaluation of the event and to help with deciding how much food and drinks to order at future events, you could keep tallies in a spreadsheet of the amount consumed and leftover of each type of food, drinks, and supplies used or unused.

## Holding a General Meeting

The purpose of a general meeting is to introduce your organization to new students and re-introduce it to existing or former members. Such meetings are common in departmentally affiliated student organizations but are not typical in student governments because their existence is usually already known, and there may be problems finding a room with a large enough capacity. Selecting a room for the meeting may involve some research, and you should check for room availability in advance either with the owning department or with the classroom scheduling office at your school. An ideal room will have an entrance near the back, so that latecomers do not interrupt the meeting. If the room you reserve is not equipped with a microphone and sound system you should try to set these up yourself, particularly if the room is large.

If possible, you should plan your General Meeting in the first few weeks of the term, because waiting until later in the term is likely to clash with midterms or finals and lead to reduced attendance. You should try to get a time when most of your target audience and board members will be available, and checking the course schedule for your department or school will help in finding times when there are no major classes occurring. Ideal times for such a meeting tends to be around lunchtime (e.g., 11 am – 1 pm), or in the evening after 5 pm. See the Appendix for an example of a useful scheduling matrix.

To attract members to the meeting, you could offer snacks or food or arrange for a guest speaker. Possible speakers include the advisor, department chair, dean, associate or assistant dean, program director, principal, or another senior administrator. Alternatively, you may invite a representative from student government or from another partner student organization. An agenda, exemplified as follows, for a general meeting to be run by the president could be posted on your organization's Web site prior to the meeting time:

**General Meeting Agenda**
1. Welcome and Call to Order
2. Introductions of Board Members and Advisor
3. Guest Speaker (if appropriate)
4. State of the Organization Address (by group's president)
5. Question and Answer Session
6. Meeting Adjournment

The meeting format would be much more flexible than a senate or board meeting, though it should start and finish on time and follow the agenda. In the Welcome and Call to Order, attendees should be welcomed to the General Meeting, asked to silence their mobile devices, and requested to raise their hand if they have questions or comments. When introducing board members, they should talk about their roles, accomplishments, and goals and make announcements about any relevant issues or activities. Most of the focus should be on promoting your organization, sharing your accomplishments and future plans, and getting feedback. Enough time should be allowed for a limited number of questions after each officer's presentation, if possible. You should introduce your guest speakers with a biographical summary and clearly outline their relationship to your organization and the reason they are speaking at your group's General Meeting. The General Meeting is a great opportunity for you to address the state of the organization outlining the vision, goals, accomplishments, and the importance of your members. In closing, you should thank your guest speaker, advisor, members, officers, and any committee members for all of their support and, finally, make sure that your group cleans up the room and vacates it by the end of the reserved time.

## Recap

You will probably employ most of these methods of publicizing your organization, if not others. Given the many different forms of media and strategies available, it is advisable to promote your organization in as many ways as possible. The ease of promotion should not mean that you have a cavalier approach to generating publicity, since careless mistakes or failure to follow school policies has the potential for embarrassment and even sanction(s), not to mention the financial irresponsibility due to wasting money on a product that cannot be used. The overall vision for promoting your organization should be to provide accurate information in a novel and memorable manner and to create a favorable impression that piques the interests of students and draws them to your group.

# Chapter 6

## How to Organize and Coordinate Programs

### Why Program?

There are many reasons to program activities and events, whether they are social, cultural, or academic in focus. Notwithstanding the major reason of attracting and keeping members, there is the opportunity to expand the horizons of your members through meeting new people and educating them about other cultures, other academic disciplines, or the community. Even when the primary focus of a student group is advocacy, organizing events can improve the visibility and increase the understanding of your organization or cause. Events provide a social outlet for students to relieve stress and build friendships, thus solidifying the basis of the organization. Activities and events also offer a great opportunity for officers of the organization to meet the members, and members can offer feedback and ideas to make the group better.

Although any program that attracts people may be considered social, some programs focus on acquiring academic knowledge, cultural awareness, community service, or networking, while some have no other agenda than simply having fun. The type of programming that your organization predominantly engages in and hence spends money on must be justified within the focus of your group. It would send conflicting messages to members and to the school community, if an organization that focused on community service primarily programs social events. Consequently, members would be entitled to question whether their funds were being spent appropriately.

### Program Planning

Adequate planning is crucial to ensuring a program's success, and planning as you go or doing little or no planning is a harbinger of failure. You should get approval for the programs you intend to host from your organization's leadership, be they a board or senate. Programming should be in line with your constitution and school policies, and programming goals should be scaled to your organization's budgetary and staffing resources, membership, and interest.

Upon approval for an event, much of the planning can be conducted at committee meetings and the following aspects should be considered:

- Type – academic, social, community service or other.

- Timing – the date and time when the event will happen.
- Attendance – how many will be expected to participate?
- Food and drinks – what will be served, if any, and how much?
- Funding – how much will need to be allocated and from what source?
- Participant cost – based on available funding, how much will the event cost to participants?
- Venue – where will the event occur?
- Prizes – what if any will be awarded and to whom?
- Advertising – how will the event be advertised?
- Supplies – what things will be needed for the event?
- Speakers – who will be presenting at the event?
- Staffing – who will be helping with the event and when?
- Management – how will the event be overseen?

Attendance at your events is critical to the perception and success of your organization. You should try to have as few conflicting dates or competing events as possible with your program schedule. Your first strategy should be to avoid religious observances and holidays, school-wide sponsored events and school holidays, or term breaks. You should also try not to schedule your events too close to each other, since students typically have diverse interests and hence a full calendar even without considering time needed to study. The danger with having events on weekends, holidays, or breaks is possible low attendance, however for residential students or other students who are typically still around when the majority are not, such programming is very valuable.

The desired frequency of programs will depend on the scale of events. One small program per week or one large program per month would be a safe target for an active organization. Back to back events can be tiring for you and your board members, and you will increase the likelihood of making mistakes by doing more than you can realistically handle. When your budget is tight, consider having programs that would cost little or no money to run.

It is very difficult to predict attendance at events, yet you must estimate the attendance in order to budget and plan effectively. To estimate attendance at a regular-type event you should research your organization's attendance history if there is one, although this will be impossible for pioneering programs and events that are being run for the first time. Using a computer-based RSVP system can be helpful, since this encourages students to place the event on their calendar and discourages no-shows after having already "committed" to the event through the RSVP. A free event planning Web site, such as www.evite.com can also be very useful, or students could simply RSVP by e-mail.

A balanced approach to programming is one that avoids a lot of repetition, by making sure your organization hosts a variety of events to appeal to a diverse student body. Even if you have had particular success with one event, hosting the same event too often during the same year or term can lead to apathy from your members. In advance, you may try to poll students on possible events to find out what interests them. However you may find yourself compelled to run an event or series of events that has been a part of a tradition lasting for many years, and if your organization does not run such events, you could face a backlash from your members. While it is inadvisable to overburden your group by trying to host too many events in a given term, having too few programs or too many unsuccessful events can lead to lower attendances, and your reputation as a leader and the reputation of your organization could suffer.

All of your programs should be safe and not pose any risk of personal injury or loss of life to the participants. Your school may require you to distribute waivers that are signed by the attendees, releasing the school and your organization from any liability due to injury resulting from participation in an activity. Because your organization is responsible for maintaining compliance with school policies, you should check with school administrators for policy documents prior to the event.

Academic events may include book discussions and readings, colloquia, conferences, forums, symposia, expositions, industry site visits, seminars, presentations, panels, lectures, and workshops. These types of events can take advantage of the resources available on school campuses including preeminent researchers, educators, and industry liaisons. Whatever the nature of your organization, it would be worthwhile to consider hosting an academic event, and there will be considerable educed respect, particularly from school administrators.

Social events may include amusement park visits, barbeques, biking, field, hiking, or ski trips, cart racing, concerts, excursions by boat, end of the term/year festivities, game tournaments, graduation celebrations, movies, museum or art exhibits, nightclubbing, socials (on campus or off campus), parties (Halloween and other holidays), plays, sport competitions, and other recreational programs. When social events are programmed well and accomplished smoothly without incident, they can serve to solidify the membership of the organization and recruit new members and leaders. Networking events are social events with a specific agenda where your organization aims to connect members with either members of other groups or with leaders in the sphere of interest of your organization to help establish contacts for internships and jobs. Mixers with faculty, staff, alumni, and other student organizations with a similar or different focus are also valuable.

Volunteer events may include collecting litter, book/toy drives, Special Olympics, tutoring in neighborhood schools, feeding the homeless, and other community or service-learning projects. These kinds of community service events with the goal of improving your neighborhood can enhance your organization's reputation, both within your school and within the community. The ensuing respect will be even greater when an organization that does not have community service as its main focus engages in such activities.

If your organization has international student members, you could program culturally-themed events with ethnic food for specially-timed occasions such as New Year celebrations or other national holidays. If possible, you should try to get assistance from students who are from that particular country to help with the details. This can be a great way for your members to become familiar with other cultures and often enriches the student experience, by providing an opportunity to meet students they may otherwise never meet.

In some instances, your organization may wish to partner with another student group to jointly program an event. This may be for any type of event, and for any number of reasons including networking, socializing, or pooling resources for a larger event than either organization could host alone. From a funding perspective, two student organizations can run a more ambitious program, and from a management perspective, extra help can be obtained for planning and staffing the event. There is also the opportunity for two student organizations from academically diverse disciplines to come together to host an interdisciplinary academic event, and joint programming with other schools (including local rivals) can make events more exciting and help students network and build friendships.

When working with other organizations, particularly those at other institutions, you should be satisfied that the group has a favorable reputation, and that they can meet their funding and publicity obligations in order to contribute to the success of the event. You will need to meet with the other organization's president and programming officer to plan the event in great detail including clearly documented roles and responsibilities, such as cost sharing. If you get the sense that the organization is not well-organized or does not communicate effectively with you, then you should reconsider joint programming with that group. There are always risks involved in joint programming, such as the risk that your organization could be left with a larger bill than was anticipated, your members would have to do the bulk of the work for the event, or unruly behavior from members of the other group could tarnish the reputation of your organization and institution.

Social mixers with faculty and staff members can be organized to help foster better relations between students and staff, and getting to know more faculty members can help students find positions working for them such as graders, research assistants, or teaching assistants. Typically, the advisor of your organization would be invited to attend events and meetings, but your group may also choose to invite other faculty or staff members to certain events. Inviting school administrators such as deans, principals, or department chairs can help with addressing issues in your organization. However, if student group money is spent on individuals who are not part of your organization, there needs to be a clear justification for doing so, especially if their attendance is subsidized or if, in the case of a limited attendance event, their presence means that a student member cannot attend.

## Publicizing Your Programs

The success of your programs will depend largely on your publicity strategy. One of the greatest challenges for an organization is to publicize the events at the beginning of the year or term when not all events have been finalized. This is especially tricky for a new programming officer or committee. It is desirable to print an information card or brochure that can be given to new students during orientation with events, dates, and venues for the entire term, but typically, there will not be enough time to plan all the events prior to printing the flyer. It is not unreasonable to have only the first month's programming pre-planned, and this schedule can be publicized fairly confidently with a note referring to the organization's Web site for subsequent program information as they are arranged. In order to save possible embarrassment, it is better not to advertise an event before securing the funding, speakers, and venue.

In any announcement, you need to provide the description, date, time, and location of the program. If there is a price to attend, then the cost needs to be mentioned as well. Popular methods of advertising include e-mail announcements to members, flyers posted around campus, announcements made at the beginning of class, or advertising in the school newspaper. Additional points on advertising are mentioned in Chapter 5.

## Selling Tickets for Events

The responsibility of your group is to program within the approved budget and, therefore, as many of your events as possible should be free to your group's members or, if applicable, to those who have paid a membership/programming fee to your organization. However, in order to have an ambitious programming schedule, there may need to be some additional funding required for an event that will need to come from those who wish to participate. This cost should be kept as low as possible and should only be a fraction of the total cost of the event, if the students were to engage in this activity on their own.

For such events, money can either be collected at the time of the event as an entry charge or collected in advance by selling tickets. The advantage of selling tickets is that you can have an approximation of how many people will be attending, and for some events with limited capacity, selling tickets or collecting non-refundable deposits are essential to avoiding disappointment and ensuring that students who say they are going to attend actually do. An example of this might be a day trip to the beach or the mountains where your organization needs to pay for a charter bus. The bus will have to be paid for regardless of how many people show up. In order to make sure that your costs are met, your programming officer could require that a non-refundable amount be deposited, or the whole ticket be purchased in order to secure a student's place on the bus. Clear instructions should be given on how and where the tickets can be purchased, and accurate records need to be kept of the students who have paid. It is important to get the e-mail addresses of the students as they sign up, in order to remind them near the time of the event and inform them of any last minute changes to the schedule. For popular events where you get more interested members than you can accommodate, you could set up a waiting list for extra or unclaimed tickets.

## Serving Food and Drinks

One major attraction to an event is free food. In fact, just providing food to your members can be an event in itself. Luncheons, dinners, and ice cream or snack socials are examples of events where food is the main attraction. If you are attending a school where the music department holds lunchtime concerts on campus, you might want to encourage your members to attend this cultural event by providing a free lunch. In this case, you could have a well-attended event without having to pay for the entertainment and merely paying for some food. There is usually an expectation that food will be provided at an event held during a normal mealtime. Holding an event during lunchtime or dinnertime without serving a meal is likely to be a recipe for disaster, since attendees may leave soon after they arrive.

Since it is difficult to estimate attendance at an open event, deciding how much food to order can be a challenge. It can be potentially quite embarrassing to run out of food at an event, although if you have a much greater turnout than reasonably expected, it is hard to avoid. You can control the consumption of food and beverages by limiting the amount given to each attendee or by supplying box lunches. It is better to have some members complain that you restricted their binging than to have other members who arrive to find that there is no food left. Of course, one of the challenges is ensuring that your members are the ones to whom food is served at an event. For events that are outdoors on campus, other students who are not affiliated with your organization may try to acquire some food, and if they are successful, there would be less available for your members. They could use phones, e-mail, or text messaging to quickly spread the word about the free food to others. This is difficult to control, and if the school identification card does not specify major or student status, it is almost impossible to control. For academically-aligned organizations, students could bring some form of enrollment verification to show their affiliation with your group, but for other groups that may not be possible. Food that is located within an enclosure, such as a roped off portion of a quad or a park, or food that is served out of the way of student foot traffic would help deter unwanted students, and only the most brazen of non-members would make the extra effort to take advantage of your free food. When an event is over, non-perishables such as unopened cans or bottles should be stored and any extra food can be given to people who help with closing after the event. Chapter 5 has more information on food, drinks, and supplies.

## Choosing a Venue

The choice and location of the venue will impact attendance at the event, especially if the venue is off campus. Selecting a venue that is too large can make attendance appear to be smaller; a venue that is too small may leave standing room only, be a fire code violation, and cause people to leave. Although gauging attendance is always a challenge, ideally, there should be adequate capacity at the venue with room for more people, if more people come than are expected. To avoid overcrowding, try to find the maximum occupancy of a place ahead of time.

When an event is on campus during the day, students would not have to think about transportation, parking, making big adjustments to their schedule, or what to wear to the event. They would just have to show up in between their academic commitments wearing what they wore to class that morning and go right back to class after the event, with minimal planning or inconvenience. By hosting an event off campus, your members will have to make significantly greater effort to attend, especially if the event is on a weekday when most of your members will typically be on campus. Typically, there has to be a big draw to attract members to an off campus event, and the event should be one that is not feasible to program on campus.

When events are held off campus, transportation becomes an issue, since many students will not have cars. So you must decide whether there is adequate public transportation and if that will be subsidized, there are enough car owners willing to carpool to cover the numbers of students expected and if your organization will subsidize fuel, or your organization provides a bus/van. When you organize transportation to an event, whether via bus/van or carpooling, your school may require passengers to sign waivers releasing the school from liability in case of an accident. Of course, there are times when your members will be responsible for their own transportation and you can provide them with a link to a Web site with public transportation information, if there is a way for them to get to and from the destination without a car. Remember that you need to consider what time your event will start and end, and try to coordinate it with the public transportation schedules.

Parking is often a major concern for members who choose to drive. If there is not enough parking available, students would be forced to park further from the event which, in some cities, could cause safety concerns. This is worth seriously considering, especially when the event finishes after dark. You might want to distribute safety tips to members, such as walking in groups, being vigilant, keeping mobile devices and wallets or purses out of sight. Your school or campus safety department may have flyers with information on personal safety. Check if there is free or validated parking for the venue and, if possible, try to reimburse event staff, special guests (e.g., speakers, presenters) for parking. Try to avoid having such attendees pay for parking altogether, if you can.

For some venues such as restaurants or theatres, you may be required to make reservations to ensure that there are enough spots for you when your group arrives. In order to reserve a venue, you may be required to pay a fee or deposit for possible damage that may or may not be refundable, and these expenses should be included in the budget for the event. If the venue serves food, you should check the health record of the site from the local health department where you should be able to find any health ratings and/or violations.

## Event Management

If your organization has a committee chair or officer responsible for the programming, then that person would typically be responsible for managing the event. If that officer/chair is not available, then another board member should be designated to supervise the event. Prior to the event time, a staff plan should be prepared to ensure that there are enough support personnel designated for event setup, management, and cleanup. Your programming officer should enlist at least two board or committee members responsible for each stage. An e-mail reminder should be sent to those helpers before the event to let them know that they must contact you immediately if they cannot come, so that replacements can be found. Those staffing the event should always maintain a positive attitude in front of others, even when things do not go according to plan, and it is important that the officer/chair responsible for the event not complain or reprimand support personnel in public. While it is important for the officers and helpers to socialize with the members at the event, they must be focused on making sure things are running according to plan and that the event starts and finishes on time. Time management is critical in staging a successful event, and enough time should be allowed between the end of the event and cleanup in order to be out of the venue by the end of the reserved time. Try to encourage as many officers, committee members, and/or senators as possible to attend your organization's events to assist with the management and meet the members.

You should also be aware of the impact of the weather on attendance. Inclement weather can discourage attendees or delay their arrival. Check the weather report ahead of time and have contingency plans, such as e-mailing an alternative indoor location for the event or having a person stationed at the pre-advertised location to direct members to the new location.

When programming on campus, you must make special effort to comply with rules on serving food and drinks in addition to smoking policies in rooms or patios. If policies forbid serving food or drinks inside buildings or in rooms, then try to serve outside or find a place where food is allowed to be served. You should have enough garbage bags and cans available, and discourage all attendees from littering. Use recycling bins, if available, and keep the venue clean and tidy throughout the event, thus making the cleanup less time-consuming after the event. Organizations that do not comply with venue policies could face disciplinary proceedings from school administrators or, at least, would not be allowed to use school facilities for future events.

## Organizing a Conference

Some student organizations host large conferences that may be called expositions or symposia. These kinds of programs can last a day or may even continue over a period of days and require a great deal of planning and a large budget. With any conference, there will be a time for the academic component, the social interaction component, and the food component (sometimes multiple meals). The logistics involved in planning for these components of a conference are equivalent to planning many discrete events, and a committee will be needed to plan and run the whole program with high overhead and many dependencies. While the conference should be overseen by an officer or a committee chair, each component should be planned by a separate subcommittee of people in order to maximize the success of the whole event. Having committee members, particularly the chair, with experience in planning a conference is invaluable for the success of the event.

**Pre-conference**

A theme of the conference should be determined and approved and the dates and approximate times should be set months in advance, probably as soon as your officers take office for the new academic year. You should have a conference Web site maintained by a designated conference committee member that contains up-to-date information such as a call for presenters, registration, and a schedule. It is advisable to hold the conference on campus or at a venue close to campus, in order to attract participants with the convenience of the location. Remember that most of the participants will be students from your school or organization, and a venue that is too far away from campus will deter participation and attendance. The venue will probably have to be reserved many months in advance, usually with a deposit.

Successful advertisement of the conference is essential. Flyers should be posted around campus and e-mail announcements should be sent out including the URL of the conference Web site. If possible, ads should be placed in your school newspaper. An impressive keynote or guest speaker will help draw a large attendance, though some high-profile distinguished speakers, administrators, or professors may require an honorarium in order to participate. The conference budget may drive the honorarium, and it may require some creative partnership with an academic or administrative unit on campus to assist with speaker fees. An impressive speaker will bring publicity to your group and probably also to your school, so do not be afraid to ask for some cost-sharing from other organizations or from academic or administrative units. Some local vendors may be attracted to help with financial support and, in return, they could be compensated by getting a table to advertise and/or link on the conference Web site. It is not recommended to charge an entry fee, since it would likely reduce attendance.

Deadlines should be set to receive all submissions (abstracts, demonstrations, presentations, and papers) and evaluation criteria, to determine which submissions will be accepted, should be established and communicated ahead of time. The deadline should be set with enough time to permit evaluation of the material by either your committee or a co-opted faculty member, in order to give enough time for the presenters to get feedback and revise their presentations.

A schedule of events for each day should also be drawn up in advance, and reliable moderators should be assigned to each session. You may decide to group presentations together based on area of study or another measure of comparison, and the schedule will be determined by the number of rooms and the length of time you have available for the conference. There may even be poster presentations and demonstrations that could be displayed in a clearly visible area. It advisable to have attendees specify which sessions they will attend at the time they register for the conference. This will give your organizing committee a sense of anticipated attendance and will help with scheduling sessions and rooms to meet the capacity.

At many conferences, food and drinks are served at breakfast, lunch, and dinner during awards times, with refreshments served during morning and afternoon breaks. Catering expenses tend to be quite high, and it is worth considering outside vendors or seeing what you could buy and serve on your own. Again, the conference budget will probably drive the decadence and variety of the food, though the campus dining service may be flexible enough to work with you on some sponsorship or discount.

## On the day of the conference

Your conference planning committee should have a team responsible for the technical aspects of the conference. The team should ensure there are enough projectors and laptop computers available for the presenters. All equipment should be tested before the conference begins and the focus, distance, and image size for any projector used should be adjusted. Contingency plans such as overhead projectors and transparencies, and back-up computers and projectors should be available in case any of the equipment fails. Before any presentation is delivered, the windows and doors should be closed to eliminate noise with the lighting adjusted and blinds closed or curtains drawn to eliminate glare on the screen.

Throughout the conference, the front registration table should be staffed at all times. Consider having name badges for all attendees with ribbons or stickers to signify presenters, conference committee members, and keynote speakers. Conference programs should also be distributed to attendees on the day of the conference. Conference awards (e.g., certificates or gifts) may be given out based on the quality of the paper, the presentations, or to those who helped with the conference. To get valuable feedback to improve future conferences, a survey could be distributed to attendees with collection boxes at the exits of the venue. Alternatively, a Web-based survey and e-mail may be sent out to participants and attendees immediately following the event.

There are many more details and logistics concerning conferences that could comprise an entire book. Planning conferences can be demanding, time-consuming, and expensive, and should not be undertaken without much consideration and support from the leadership of your organization. There is a large outlay of time and money on planning, logistics, finding speakers, presenters and panelists, often requiring a large staff to manage the high communication overhead and a busy schedule.

## Debriefing

As soon after your events as possible, while still fresh in everyone's minds, the board/committee should sit down and debrief in order to find out what went right and wrong. In this post-program analysis, you should get feedback from board members who participated and analyze any surveys you administered to participants. Typical measures of the success of a program include attendance, budget overruns, cost per attendee, measured or perceived satisfaction, and the amount of leftover food and drinks. For analysis purposes, you will need to remember to record the number of members who attend each event. Even an estimate of the average of the reported count by board members collectively will suffice. By tracking attendance in a historical database, you have ideas of possible attendance by venue that can assist future officers and committees in their planning. For those events which required a sign-up or RSVP, the percentage of no-shows should also be recorded.

A large part of programming is experimental, so do not lose hope if there is low attendance at one of your events. If those who attended believe their time and money was not wasted, and that the planning committee budgeted and planned effectively, word will get around and the reputation of your organization will increase leading to greater attendance at future events.

# Chapter 7

# How to Get Feedback and Address Issues of Members

## Purpose of Student Advocacy

Your primary role as an elected student leader is to represent the constituents who have put their faith in you by voting for you. You are a public servant. The main problem facing you is that because you are a student you do not make school policy. School policies are made by administrators, often after many months or years of deliberation and consultation. Policies are almost always adopted based on sound reasoning and evidence, by people who are committed to the institution and want an effective administrative structure within which to work. They are not made lightly. Policies usually end up in an official printed document that can only be changed every one or two years, depending on the printing cycle. It is worth noting that even administrators cannot change their own policies easily. Therefore, to enter the arena as a student leader, with your role to bring about effective change for the betterment of your constituents requires patience, long-term thinking and goals, and an attitude of collaboration with those who can change policy. You also need to have justified reasons for wanting to bring about changes in the school environment, and those reasons are to be found in the voice of the students. The point of student advocacy is to make a valuable contribution to your school and members through drawing the attention of administrators to various academic or student life concerns. Departmental organizations should try to work with their student government to address issues and concerns beyond the domain of their own members. Student governments tend to have more power and influence on a school's administration than the groups beneath them. Eventually, these ideas would then be submitted to administrators through the student government. Successful leaders will continually be in touch with their constituents, but a leader who is most effective in bringing about change will have firm evidence of the concerns of the students to bring before the administration. This requires a lot of hard work, strategic planning, well-grounded infrastructure, and some objective data–not unlike a research project.

## Forming Committees

One of the most vital components of student organizational infrastructure is the committee, and one of the greatest means of addressing issues is through forming committees to deal with the concerns of your members. Committees are typically listed in the organization's bylaws as either standing or ad hoc. Standing committees are expected to be a fixture of the organization and to be busily and consistently working on student concerns or interests. Ad hoc committees are designed to be set up in response to a particular issue as it arises. For each committee, there is the expectation of a mid-year and an end-of-year report to the board or senate. This means that work has to get done. Committees need strong leadership and committed members. They are typically all volunteers deeply concerned about a particular student issue. Volunteers who are giving of their precious time need to see specific goals and determined progress towards those goals, if they are to remain engaged. As leader of your student organization, you should spend some time thinking about whom you will ask to chair the committees, and you should try to schedule regular meetings with the chairs and always be available as needed. If your budget can absorb it, you should ensure that your organization has committee allowance as a line item and that each committee chair has access to a procurement card (for refreshments, etc.) for the entire committee each time they meet. This will help the committee members feel appreciated, improve attendance, and contribute greatly to a hardworking results-driven team. Committees of all sizes need some organizational structure with responsibility assigned to members for certain jobs or roles. Typically there is a chair, and other positions could include a communications director to take the minutes, a vice chair, and positions responsible for publicity, recruitment, data analysis, technology, etc.

Committee goals need to be formally targeted to address an established pervasive concern, in the case of a standing committee, or a novel acute concern, in the case of an ad hoc committee. It is important therefore to reach out to those your organization represents, who elected you as their advocate, to understand the issues facing them and seek possible resolution. There are a number of means for getting feedback from members such as through focus groups, discussion groups, task forces, town hall meetings, and forums. However, one of the best ways of doing this is to administer a survey. A standing committee will most likely be composed of students who have an interest and are informed about a particular issue. These committee members will know what questions need to be included in the survey based on their experience and understanding of the issue. Often, surveys validate what you may anecdotally be aware of, and although most administrators are reluctant to pursue policy changes based on anecdotal evidence, the results of a valid survey can be very convincing. The committee should select a modest number of questions that gather as much information as possible in as little time as possible.

## Writing a Survey

It might be easy for a school administrator to ignore the complaints of one or two students, but to ignore the collective or representative voice is unwise. Your job is to gather evidence from the collective voice in a valid and reliable manner and present the findings to the administration. The results of a survey will inform you of the concerns of your constituents and will form the basis of your advocacy platform. If you are to have any influence with the school administration, you will need to have a thorough survey to justify your advocacy. Remember that many of the top administrators at reputable schools are recruited from the research community, and they will have made careers from gathering and interpreting data. It will not be an easy sell unless your data collection is performed in a respected manner.

Questionnaires can be very frustrating to administer because of the challenges involved in getting people to respond. It is important to have a surveying structure for your organization that will transcend several boards and student leaders. There should be as few surveys administered as possible per year to a given population. However, your survey strategy should determine that annual surveys are administered to targeted subsets of the student body or to a random sample that represents the whole constituency. Because there is typically greater turnaround in student leadership than in school administration, it is worth having a surveying philosophy and strategy that is embraced by each new student leader, so that general advocacy through the standing committees can be sustained through the years. You can be certain that if you over-survey a population you will have a very low response rate, and that is bad for your advocacy.

Because surveys are anonymous, you can avoid personal questions, though some indication of the field of study or degree sought by the student answering the questionnaire can be very helpful in analyzing the locale of the problem and targeting resources. Other demographic questions may include number of years in the school or program and whether the student is domestic or international.

You should keep the smaller surveys to around a dozen or so questions with a range of answers on a five-point scale (Likert) and one or two open-ended answers. Likert scales and open-ended answers give more room for interpretation of the data than simple true/false or agree/disagree type answers. They also allow students to express their views more comprehensively and will contribute to your greater understanding of the issue. It is more likely that students will complete a question where one of the answer choices accurately reflects their opinion, rather than being forced to make a one-of-two choice answer. There is also more validity in an answer of "strongly agree" on a scale with answer choices of "strongly disagree, disagree, neutral, agree, strongly agree," than an answer of "agree" on a choice of "agree or disagree."

It is recommended to include some questions that address academic issues as well as student life issues surrounding the problem with which the standing committee is concerned. For example, a campus safety standing committee might ask questions about how safe people feel on campus at night and how that impacts their study habits and their social lives. Students who don't feel safe on campus at night may be less inclined to walk home from a party at night, but they may also be reluctant to work late in the lab or in the library. This impediment to academic pursuit would be a troubling finding and one that administrators might want to address by allocating more resources to campus safety. Recognizing that many administrators are from the ranks of faculty, a campus culture that promotes academic activities is well understood and anything that you can do to survey the population and gather data on that facet of student life will be of great interest to the administration, especially where they can change policy to make a positive impact on academics. Sample surveys are included in the Appendix.

## Administering a Survey

Nowadays, there are many companies that offer free surveying tools placing survey design and administration within reach of almost every organization. These sites also present your results in a tabular form for easy analysis. Publicizing the survey can be difficult. Some schools may not share their student e-mail database with an organization to mass-e-mail the student population, which is why it is worthwhile to build a database of names and e-mail addresses at your recruiting/social events. You should announce the survey by e-mail to as many of your constituents as you can, and ask the student organization leaders and senators to publicize it at their meetings and in their classes. Whenever possible, you should send weekly reminders to those who have not yet completed it, gently reminding them of the importance of the survey and the benefits of having a large response rate.

## Rewards as Incentives

In the busy life of a student, time is often too precious to be spent in answering questionnaires, even ones that don't require too much time and effort, such as an electronically administered survey. You will need a budget to administer a survey, and you should offer as many valuable prizes as possible in order to encourage completion. If the survey is to be administered over a number of weeks, you might offer one or two prizes per week. This may encourage and benefit early responders who would be in the draw for more prizes than late responders. Alternatively, you might want to have a number of prizes of increasing value that are administered at the same time after the conclusion of the survey. You might even be able to get sponsorship of the prizes from, say, the campus bookstore, a dining facility, or the school ticket office. You should publicize the winners so that the surveyed population knows that prizes were actually awarded, and the better the prizes, the more likely you are to have a greater number of responders. It is a small price to pay for a large data set with which you can advocate and is also a justifiable use of your organization's budget.

## Data Analysis

Since time is a precious commodity in the life of a student, it is important that you make effective use of every question and make an initial analysis of each of them. You will probably want to present the demographic data in the form of a bar graph or pie chart, and you should present the response rate and the distribution of answers both as a percentage and as raw numbers. Do not be afraid to be honest about the number of responses received. Even with a low response rate, valuable insight can still be gained from the study. Once you can see the data and how the answers inform you about the issue, you can begin to form the basis of your report. It is advisable to present the raw data in tabular or figural form, clearly discernable by question, either within the body of the report or as an appendix. Remember that some administrators will be very interested in the data itself as well as your interpretation of the data in the report.

## Making a Report

Since you will be presenting the raw data to the reader, it is somewhat moot and boring for the text to simply reiterate the data, answer by answer. A clever strategy is to present an overview of the data set as a whole, using the individual question data to support a point you need to make. Presenting your data set embedded in the report itself rather than as an appendix helps with the flow of the report. You should tailor the text within the report towards your particular hypothesis or reason for conducting the study in the first place. The more you can generalize your statements and formulate a consensus from among a number of questions, the more likely an administrator and your colleagues will be to read it. It is also important to have order throughout the report. The key components of a report are a title page, a summary, an introduction, the methods used, the results and discussion, a conclusion and list of recommendations, and, finally, a list of the resources used. These components are explained in the following sections.

## Title Page

The title page should contain the title of your report, the author or the committee that administered it, and the name of the student organization, followed by the date of the report.

## Summary

This will be a separate page that contains a 300-500 word summary including the reason for the survey, the population surveyed, the major findings and the recommendations. It is an overview without specifics; the specifics will be in the report itself. A well-written summary will whet the appetite of the readers, compelling them to take a deeper look at the data and the expanded discussion and conclusions.

## Introduction

Begin with an introduction to the reason for the study and what events or anecdotal evidence led this to be of significant importance to merit the work involved in administering a survey. Also, include a brief introduction to the student organization and the size of the represented constituency within the school. In other words, the reader should know who administered the survey, who was surveyed, and why that group was targeted. Your introduction should end with clearly stated aims and objectives of the study. Some people even prefer to have a short section dedicated to aims and objectives.

## Methods

In this section you should include a detailed description of the way the survey was administered, the tools used, the length of time the survey was live, the number of questions and how they were chosen, the prizes offered and methods of analysis, and statistics used, if any. This is your chance to be credible. A well-chosen methodology will contribute greatly to the integrity of the report and hence your ability to use the data for advocacy.

## Results and Discussion

Begin this section by informing the reader of the number of people in the whole population you are trying to gather data on, then the number of people who were targeted to respond to the questionnaire, and, finally, the number of people who actually completed the survey. These numbers should also be presented in a percentage format. For example, if your student body is 2,000 strong and you send the survey to 500 people, you would report as your strategy surveying 25% of the population. If 250 responded, your response rate would be 50% and you then present your data as a percentage of the responders, i.e., a percentage of 250 students. Therefore, if 200 students reported a difficulty in making the transition to your institution, you would present that as "80% of the students surveyed experienced a difficult transition to our school." In this section, you have the opportunity to be impressive with your use of embedded tables and figures that present the data in a clear and simple manner. Selective use of color (or contrasting shading if you are photocopying/printing the report in black and white) can help distinguish between groups or answers where necessary. You can use percentages in the discussion of the data, and where possible you should try to discuss how your collected data relates to your original concerns and reasons for undertaking the survey. It should also lead easily to the formation of logical recommendations that arise directly as a result of the perceived problem and the data that speaks to the issue. Where answers indicate that the school administration is, in fact, doing a satisfactory job, you should not be afraid to highlight these and balance them in the light of other data where improvements can be made. As an advocate, you are much more likely to meet with a more willing administration where they are rightfully acknowledged for the beneficial work they are trying to do for students. You should try to be non-biased in your discussion of the results and avoid using emotionally charged words or phrases. Remember that the administration will be expected to have read the report before they meet with you to discuss the issues you addressed. If you present a thoughtful discussion of the data, you are more likely to be treated seriously and to be met with a spirit of cooperation than if your report is charged with venom!

## Conclusions and Recommendations

The conclusions and recommendations are another opportunity for you and your organization to gain an honorable reputation. Thoughtful and carefully worded recommendations that are attainable will help garner the support you will need in order for those changes to be made. If a change in policy or practice is recommended and sufficient justification is presented from the data, then people are more likely to offer their resources or help in making the necessary adjustments. This section should encapsulate the report along with the introduction, and these two sections should provide an overview of the whole study. The conclusions will reflect the outcome of the discussion and lead to recommendations to address the issues raised through initiatives at the organization level or the school administration level. Remember that the purpose of the survey is to identify how to improve student life rather than to expose the administration, and the data may even call for a change in the way student leaders fulfill their responsibilities. Partnership with the administration works very well, and recommendations that bear the responsibility of the student leader as well as recommendations that fall within the purview of the administration will gain more allegiance than recommendations that are solely directed at the shortcomings of the school administration.

## Resources Used

If you have used some national norms or some reports from a newspaper, including your school newspaper, or even from the Internet, it is important for you to reference the sources used either as a bibliography or in the text. This not only shows responsible use of other people's literature but also shows that you have researched the topic in justifying your decision to administer a survey.

## Approving Recommendations

Once you have written your report and arrived at the recommendations, the committee will have to vote on approving the recommendations for presentation to the board or senate. The appropriate board should then vote to approve the recommendations contained in the report and, subsequently, the student leader should officially circulate the report to the school administrators who are stakeholders in the issues that have been addressed.

## Circulating the Report

This report, while conducted at the committee level, has now become an officially adopted document by the organization and, as such, represents the constituency. It should be presented to the administration for their review with an official memo from the president of the organization and, if applicable, the committee chair. The memo should be written on the official letterhead of your student organization, addressed to all of the intended recipients (include their titles), and include a brief statement of what they are receiving. A sample memo is included in the Appendix.

## Collaborating with the Administration on a Large Survey

Most large schools have an office of student research charged with surveying students on an annual basis or other regular time frame. These surveys are often long and take a lot of time to complete but generate a tremendous amount of useful data. If you have the opportunity to partner with such an office and commit some of your budget for a large and comprehensive survey, you could generate some very interesting data about your constituents. The results of such a survey will have much greater efficacy than any small-scale survey that your organization has the time and resources to administer alone. Partnering with school officials will raise your profile within the academic institution and also give the administration more ownership of the results with a vested interest in addressing any concerns raised. However, notwithstanding a promising relationship with the administration, there could be some control issues in this type of partnership. It could be that not all the questions that you want are included in the survey, it may be that you don't get to see the complete data set until after the other stakeholders have seen it, and/or it may be that you don't get to write the report. Nevertheless, the benefits outweigh the potential problems, and a large comprehensive survey of your constituents will always be useful in advocacy.

# Chapter 8

## How to Relate to and Negotiate with Administrators

### 10 Tips for Success with Administrators

One of the privileges of being a student leader is the access you have to key school officials. Often, you will have access to the big decision makers at your institution. In your role as representative of the student body, it is your responsibility to use these opportunities to advance the issues you have been elected to address. The key to a successful year as a student leader is to develop successful working relationships with the policy makers of the institution. Without their support, your accomplishments will be limited to implementing programs that can be initiated through your own budget and do not need support from administrators. While social and academic programming is important, it cannot take the place of advocacy and pushing for changes in policy. If you are inheriting the reins of a student organization that has a history of successful relationships with school administrators, you will already be at an advantage. Administrators will be expecting you to continue the strong legacy and will be keen to assist you where they can. You may even have inherited some ongoing advocacy from your predecessor, and you will need to meet with expectant administrators to finish the work. However, if your predecessor created fractious relationships with the school administration, you should be prepared to start over and work hard to earn their trust and goodwill.

You can reasonably expect that an administrator will be willing to meet with a student leader at least once. However, it should be your goal to create a relationship where the administrator is not only fulfilling an obligation but is actually looking forward to meeting with you again, thus providing you with multiple opportunities to advance student issues. The more you can do to create a positive relationship with the decision making administrators the more success you will have as an advocate. Although individual administrators may have vastly different areas of responsibility and may work in different parts of the campus, they often interact with each other, especially those who are higher up in the administration. It will be very beneficial to you, your organization, and your successor if you can create a positive buzz among the administrators, so that when they converse with each other, they have great things to say about you. This will further enhance your effectiveness and increase your chances of generating new relationships and being successful in a broad scope of advocacy. Ten tips for making a positive impression and for creating and maintaining a strong relationship with an administrator are presented in this chapter.

## Tip 1: Converse with the Top of the Totem Pole

The top of the totem pole is usually where the head is found along with the decision making capabilities. This is where you, the student leader, want your advocacy agenda to be heard. You can't afford the extra time it takes to talk to administrators who can only say "that sounds like a good idea, I'll have to present it to (the dean or the vice president or the vice provost) and get back to you." Student leadership consumes a lot of time, and you are primarily at school to get a degree or for another educational endeavor. You don't want your studies to suffer because you are spending too much time on your student leadership activities. You also have limited time to fulfill the promises you made to your constituents at the time of your election, whether your term in leadership is limited by the constitution or by the need to graduate. It is not helpful for you to talk to someone who has to talk to someone else, who has to get back to the first person, and who then has to get back to you. In academic administration, getting back to someone is sometimes a lengthy process. There are many priorities consuming the top administrators and to add another level of administration into the equation convolutes the communication line. Try to go to the top yourself. Present your own case and hear an immediate answer from someone who can actually make the decision. It is harder for the decision maker to say "no" to your face, than it is to say "no" to a subordinate who may not have presented your case properly in the first place. Find out who has ultimate authority in the area where you see the need for advocacy, and ask for a meeting. You should not be surprised to have your request granted. After all, you are an elected representative, and it behooves a highly ranked school administrator to meet with and listen to the concerns of one who speaks on behalf of many others. This is how things get done: Face-to-face meetings, building relationships, and the opportunity to present a clear case for advocacy with those who have the authority to make decisions. When you go to the top, you may get directed back to a lower administrator, but you then go to them at the direction of their boss, and that is certainly a better place to be in negotiations.

## Tip 2: Know What You Want to Accomplish and How They Can Help

Your time in leadership is precious, and you shouldn't waste it. The time of academic administrators is also precious, especially the higher-ups. You do not want to waste their time, either by arranging a meeting to make a point that you haven't thought through or in order to get face-time. Arranging a meeting without having a substantial agenda is detrimental to having a successful relationship with the administration and to having a productive year as a student leader. You will lose credibility before you have even started. If you are inheriting a solid organization that has elected commendable leaders in the past, then there is probably a legacy of lasting relationships with administrators and a history of successful advocacy. Certain aspects of student life are very difficult to change at all, let alone in one student leader's term. You may be following up on an advocacy issue of your predecessors, and you may have some of your own. You will have set goals to accomplish based on your passions, your election promises, and the leanings of your board or senate. When it comes to meeting with administrators for the first time, let them know what is on your agenda, how you intend to transition issues from the previous leadership, and exactly how you might want to invite them to be involved. By inviting them to be involved, you are building collegiality which is the best tactic for success and begets the most rewarding relationships. It is important that you research the areas of responsibility under the purview of the administrator with whom you plan to meet, and then determine exactly how you both can partner together to overcome a particular problem. Write down and prioritize a list of items to discuss and have this list with you when you talk with administrators, making sure you get as much discussed as possible. Meeting an administrator with a solid and well-thought-out agenda is a harbinger of a productive year ahead in student leadership.

## Tip 3: Dress Appropriately

You've often heard it: first impressions are very important. As a student, you are not expected to dress professionally day-to-day, but you should do so for meetings with administrators. This may prove challenging at times, and may mean bringing dress clothes to school to wear for a couple of hours in the day or even for a single short meeting. If your student organization has an office, you could hang your dress clothes on the door and change right before the meeting and change back right afterwards as you go to your next class. Since many of the higher administrators come from the faculty, they are well aware of how the typical student dresses for classes. Surely, they will appreciate the trouble you have gone through in making the effort to respect the occasion by changing into more professional clothes, and doing so gives you more credibility. Administrators are also aware that students are typically on a limited budget during their schooling, and you would certainly be excused wearing the same outfit to many different meetings as long as the clothes are clean!

## Tip 4: Arrange for a Meeting

Sometimes as a student leader you will have the opportunity to attend high profile events, such as Trustees', President's or Alumni Association meetings where you will rub shoulders with key academic administrators. At such high profile meetings you may well be the only student in the room, and probably the key administrators will guess that you must be pretty important to have been invited and will be keen to talk to you. This is a great opportunity for you to casually mention that you might like to meet with them at a convenient time to talk about a student issue that is within their purview. They will almost always hand you a business card and invite you to contact them directly or contact their assistant, and this you must do. Gather the information on the issues you wish to discuss and arrange a meeting. If you get no response, check to make sure that they are not out of town or very busy with a report that may be due to the school chancellor, president, or principal the following day. This information can usually be gathered from some of their direct reports with whom you may have developed a relationship. If they are not out of town or not exceptionally busy and have not replied within three days, then you should follow up with another e-mail or even pay a visit to their assistant to make sure you get on the administrator's calendar. You will usually find that their failure to reply was an oversight and that they are very glad that you persisted with a follow-up. If you don't follow up, it may send a message that you were not serious about the meeting in the first place. If you have any qualms about being persistent or perceived as annoying, remember that you owe it to those who elected you to try hard to meet those administrators who make policy to advance their cause.

## Tip 5: Be Nice

No doubt you have been elected as a student leader because of your passion for improving the quality of education and life for your constituents. Passion is necessary to accomplish the goals you have set for your year as a leader, but in an academic institution, having passion must be tempered by the ability to win support from those who can make changes. Passion that is not well counterbalanced by affability can alienate the very ones you need to be engaging. As the old saying goes, "you catch more flies with honey than vinegar." Indeed, administrators are likely to want to assist with the success of an initiative if it is presented to them in a rational and respectful manner. Meeting administrators with a chip on your shoulder or while trying to impose an obligation on them makes it difficult for them to want to help you, even if they think your issue has merit.

## Tip 6: Ask for Help in Private

A tactful strategy is to give administrators a way to say "no" without embarrassing either themselves or you. This is easily done in private in an office or over coffee or lunch. You need to have an effective sales pitch, to ask for their help and to be prepared to graciously accept a decline. Do not worry, there may be other ways they can help later, and you don't want to ruin a relationship by making it difficult for them to say no. If you find yourself discussing your ideas with administrators in a public setting, and you think they may be able to help, don't be tempted to ask them to commit to helping your cause at that time. Instead, ask them if you could schedule a meeting to talk about the issue in more depth at a later date. Such an approach is non-threatening enough so as to lead to a great opportunity for you to advocate and to permit the administrator to let you know what they can or can't do. Contrary to what some student leaders may think, administrators really do have boundaries, even the ones at the top of the totem pole, so be mindful of that and be prepared to work within the limits of what is possible.

## Tip 7: Work Hard and Delegate When You Can

You have been elected to represent the interests of the student body and to lead a group of other elected officials and volunteers. No matter how hardworking you are, you will have to delegate in order to accomplish your goals. You will need to delegate some tasks, so that you can free yourself up to work on initiatives that involve direct partnership with school administrators. When you delegate tasks to your officers, establish agreed-upon timelines and outcomes and make sure you follow up regularly. When you meet with an administrator, you must be the one to drive the initiative forward and work as hard as you can to bring about the change in policy you are seeking. In some cases, the administrators will be willing to bear a large part of the workload. In other cases, they will expect all the work to be done by you, and their contribution will be to sign off on the policy or initiative. That alone is worth some really hard work on your part. You should be prepared to be the one who does all the work and demonstrate your willingness to take responsibility early on. You should also follow up regularly with the administrators informing them of your progress, asking for their input when you need it and even sometimes when you do not! While it can be very time-consuming to work on initiatives that result in changes in school policy, it is also a tremendous privilege to have the opportunity to work with a school administrator. Not many students ever have that opportunity. It is your chance to make a meaningful change that will benefit a myriad of students. It is also your chance to earn their respect by your dedication and tenacity and to elevate the status of your organization through your demonstrated work ethic.

## Tip 8: Dream Big and Don't be Deterred by the Fear of Failure

Few students ever lead a student organization. It is a wonderful opportunity to experience the inner workings of an academic institution and to do something beneficial for your fellow students. With this chance, you can either play it safe or you can take risks that will either result in revolutionary success or dramatic failure. If you have a vision of an ambitious plan that would really make a difference in students' lives but would cost a lot of money and involve the support of several key administrators and may not work, you need to decide whether it is worth the risk to pursue it or not. This will be somewhat determined by whether you are risk-averse by nature, whether you are ambitious or not, and whether you believe it is a justifiable use of your time and energy in representing those who elected you.

When taking risks, you put your reputation on the line and, to some extent, the reputation of your student organization. Taking risks is one of the most exciting aspects of the role as a student leader. If you take risks merely to make the headlines, you probably will make the headlines, though perhaps not as you had intended! If you take measured risks because you are willing to put your reputation on the line and to work hard for something that will greatly improve student life, and if you are willing to start an initiative that may have to be completed by, and possibly credited to, your successor, then there is a lot to be gained by taking the risk, even if it results in failure. Some risks can be taken within the scope of the student organization and involve your own time, money, and resources. Other risks involve the time, money, resources, and reputation of school administrators, and they tend to be conservative in their role. Thus, your enthusiasm, reputation, forethought, along with the potential payoff of the initiative all combine, in order to get support from administrators who also must consider their own reputation with their superiors and colleagues.

Most really big decisions and the ones that involve the most risk are made by a board or trustees of the institution, rather than the administration. However, administrators with a budget usually have the authority to spend it as they see fit, though they will have to account for it at the end of the fiscal year. Therefore, given the right circumstances and a demonstration of need, an administrator may be willing to take a measured risk as a result of your advocacy.

For example, if you have heard anecdotally that students do not want to study in the library late at night because they are afraid to walk around campus after dark, you might choose to address this as a student leader.

Your proposed solution might involve extra security patrols around the library and residential areas, in addition to the establishment of a shuttle service from the library to the residence halls. Thus, you would need to meet with administrators in the campus safety division and the transportation division to share your concern and proposed remedy. Increasing security patrols would cost money, whether hiring a new security guard or paying a current guard overtime. Providing a shuttle service might involve buying a vehicle, or if a vehicle already exists, the additional cost of a driver, gas, and wear and tear of the vehicle. Neither of the administrative units is likely going to put out that kind of money, especially if it wasn't in the budget at the start of the fiscal year. Even if they agree that it is a wise idea, they would have to take money from elsewhere in their budgets to fund these initiatives. They are also unlikely to agree to help you without a convincing argument. The collective voice of the student body is a powerful bargaining tool; however, you need to harness that voice. Short of asking students to flood the inbox of the administrators with e-mails asking for the services, which would not be very popular with them, a student survey is the only other realistic method of gathering comprehensive data to support your advocacy. In order to pursue your advocacy and convince the administrators to take a measured risk involving real money, you will have to do the hard work of gathering survey data. See Chapter 7 for more information about surveys.

Let us suppose that you have administered the survey and the data overwhelmingly indicates that students say they would study more in the library late at night with extra security and a shuttle service. You still do not know if there actually will be an increased number of students in the library at night, if the new initiatives are put in place. This is where the risk is to you, as a student representative, asking for administrators to allocate their resources in line with your identified need. If the end result is that students still do not study in the library late at night, then the perception is that the money has been wasted on your advocacy, and that is a detriment to working with administrators in the future. Your willingness to assume some of the financial risk will serve to convince the administrators that you are serious in your advocacy and increase their likelihood of supporting your request. If your budget permits, you might ask your board/senate to approve an allocation to cover the cost of gas for a term for the new shuttle service.

You need not be undone by the fear of failure if you have determined that the cause is worth pursuing, done your research, and put enough resources into the initiative to allow it to succeed. With these prerequisites, administrators are more likely to partner with you and to assume their own measured risk. If the agreement is to reassess the success of the initiative after a term or year, then the amount of resources risked is decreased somewhat. Some really fruitful initiatives may begin slowly or may have seemed as if they were going to fail. Measured risk-taking, when the sole purpose of the risk is for the betterment of the student body, is an opportunity that a student leader will have.

## Tip 9: Say "Thank you" in Public

Perhaps the best thing you can do as a student leader is to say "thank you" to an administrator in public, and a big "thank you" at that. If administrators have taken ownership with you of a project, they have probably put at least a portion of their reputation on the line and a lot of their time and effort. This deserves gratitude, even if the outcome is not quite as you imagined. Administrative units in schools often move very slowly, some would say at glacial pace, and to get anything changed or accomplished within a year or your term limit should be seen as a success. Hence, make sure you thank the administrator who has helped you. There are a few thank-you strategies that will be well received.

Whenever you achieve something in which you partner with administrators, send a letter of thanks to the administrators and copy their supervisor and some of their peers with whom you have also worked closely. This has the multiple effect of publicly announcing your accomplishment, thanking the administrator for help, and informing the general administrative leadership that you have been successful in other areas of advocacy and you appreciate administrator partnership. Whenever a report on an initiative is desired, you should send copies of it to the institutional leadership with an accompanying memo summarizing the report and thanking the administrators involved for their help. You might want to order thank-you cards and regularly send them to administrators for everything from simply meeting with you to helping you out, and you should encourage your board to do the same. Make it a hallmark of your leadership to be remembered as the thankful student leader. If your budget permits, you should make it a point to take one key administrator out to lunch per month.

Whenever administrators come to speak to your board or senate meetings, you should introduce them by recapping their help in any of your initiatives and causes, so that the officers or senators would have the opportunity to applaud them and appreciate their presentation all the more. It will also put many of them at ease with a friendly welcome. If you have an end-of-year awards ceremony to celebrate your achievements, you might want to invite all the top administrators to join you for the event. Along with honoring student leaders and groups, you might want to honor one or two administrators with professionally made certificates of appreciation or other awards for their dedication to students. Finally, if you produce an end-of-year report highlighting your successful year of advocacy and programming, you should mention all administrators (whatever their level) who have helped you throughout the year and send them a copy. Generally, administrators appreciate having their name associated with beneficial advocacy and advancing student issues. Finally, saying "thank you" to people means that they are more likely to be available to help you and your successors on future issues.

## Tip 10: Keep Yourself Continually in Their Thoughts

A legitimate goal of your time in student leadership would be to raise the profile of your organization with the top school administrators. They all should know that your organization exists, but not too many will necessarily know more than that. Your group could have a public relations budget that covers the purchase of gifts, trinkets, and other useful items branded with your organization's logo to distribute to students, especially new ones. You will probably have ordered relatively inexpensive items in bulk, such as pens, t-shirts, mugs, insulated travel mugs, bottle opener key chains, LED key chains, and tricolor highlighters all with your organization's name, logo, and Web site on them. You should not overlook administrators as you distribute these publicity items. Each time you have a high profile school committee meeting, you should take a small gift for all of the committee members. Every month, your officer/chair responsible for public relations could assemble small goody bags for a host of administrators to keep them mindful of your organization. Administrators appreciate the thought and the novelty of receiving thoughtful items including small fun gifts, your annual reports, and thank-you letters and cards. You should manage to send something to the administrators at least every month or term, and that will always be an easy way to begin a conversation when you next meet them.

Developing a successful relationship with the school administration is the most important accomplishment for a student leader with a mandate to advocate for changes in policy. The demonstration of a relentless pursuit of improvement in the quality of student life through hard work, partnership with administrators, and investment of your own resources in response to a documented need will earn the respect of the administration. Engaging school administrators through your demonstrated integrity and gratitude will serve to cement the place of your student group in the administrative fabric of the institution, helping ensure your success and the success of subsequent leaders in your organization.

# Chapter 9

# How to Carry Out Elections, Transitions, and Training

## Elections

One of the most eagerly anticipated events in the student organization calendar is the annual election. The new officers can significantly shape the organization and make a big impact on school administrators and improve campus life for the student body. Students who are passionate about student issues or representation and who are in adequate academic standing should have the opportunity to take part in the election process. From the perspective of the organization, the more there are of students who run in an election, the better the chances of strong and effective leadership from the board. A successful election begins with effective recruiting that starts very early. The officer and/or committee responsible for recruiting should be shamelessly promoting the annual election almost from the time they begin to serve. The health of the student organization depends on a competitive and enthusiastic election with a large percentage of voter turnout. Therefore, the recruitment officer/committee has a huge responsibility for promoting the conditions that will ensure an election consisting of as many qualified candidates as possible, in order to ensure the effectiveness of the organization in the following year. It is also important to have a legitimate and ethical election with a judiciary or election committee standing by to hear any complaints about the conduct of candidates or canvassers. It is in the interests of all parties implicitly or directly involved with the organization to have an ethical election. In too many instances, candidates have embarrassed themselves, their organization, and the school by resorting to unethical practices in order to get ahead. Regularly, pages of student newspapers are covered with allegations of misconduct, bending the rules, and reports of sanctions against campaigns or candidates at election time. While a student government or group is somewhat of a small stage in terms of political leadership, it is, nevertheless, a stage where people are watching. Student newspapers are read far and wide by alumni, local and sometimes national press, and students from other schools.

While the recruitment officer/committee cannot control the behavior of the candidates or their campaign strategies, they have the duty to ensure that all candidates know the election rules and policies, and possible sanctions for failing to campaign within those boundaries. Any allegations of misconduct should be heard by the judiciary or election committee and sanctions should be immediately applied when violations have occurred. School administrators and faculty are also watching the election process, and such a public occasion is a great opportunity to earn respect. For many reasons, it is worthwhile for candidates to play fair and ensure an ethical and healthy election.

## Preparing for the Election

The recruitment officer/committee will need to work closely with the officer/committee for public relations to organize and publicize a number of information seminars, detailing the elections process and candidly outlining the roles and responsibilities of each position that is up for contention. People who intend to run in the election should not be involved in the election or recruitment committee. It is highly likely that many candidates will be self-identified by their passion for certain programming or for advocacy, their leadership qualities, and their informal shadowing and supporting of elected officers, as they perform their duties. The more challenging part of the recruitment effort is to provide the opportunity for other students to get involved in the election and to encourage them to run. All elected officers should be available to talk about their roles and responsibilities. The recruitment officer or committee should publicize the office hours or contact info of the officers currently holding positions, in order for interested students to get an understanding of the expectations and time commitment required. This is especially important to encourage new people to consider running for office. The public relations officer/committee will need to publicize the opportunity to run via their listserv or mailing list, in newsletters, on the Web site, and/or through flyers posted around campus. Any budget that was approved for the purposes of recruitment can be used for refreshments at these information sessions and for publication of election ballots, where used, or voting guides.

The timing of the election is important to consider. With an election in the spring term, summer can be reserved for a transition period. However, impromptu elections may be necessary if any officers leave their position unexpectedly. Obviously there will need to be a deadline by which all candidates will have to declare their intent to run. This could be about two months prior to the last meeting of the term, the meeting at which the election results would be announced. Your organization can establish recommended qualifications for positions, such as having previously served on a committee within your group, or having been a member for at least a year. The intent to run should be submitted by a paper or an online application filed or e-mail sent by the students indicating their full name, school ID number, the position for which they are running, a statement that they are familiar with the election policies and will abide by them, and an agreement that should they be elected they will fulfill the requirements of their position with integrity and adherence to school policies. The candidate could also have the opportunity to submit a campaigning statement that could be hosted on the student organization's Web site, so that students and senators can get an idea of the candidates for whom they would like to vote. In the interests of space and readability, it is worth considering a word limit. It is also possible for the student organization to host a streaming campaign video from the candidates to make the message a little more personal. This message should be time-limited and may depend upon server space and available resources. The statement of purpose for candidates could include a summary of their background, qualifications, achievements, contributions, involvement, and goals associated with the student organization.

## Running an Election

Depending upon whether your constitution demands that elections be decided by the whole student membership or by a senate, there will be different considerations. For constituent-based voting, campaigning is a much bigger deal in this type of election, and it is likely that candidates will have teams and a strategy for publicizing their case. Inevitably, there will be school-wide rules that apply to every student organization, such as policies on posting flyers and placards, free speech areas, and tabling reservation policies. There could also be rules imposed by the student organization such as a window of time for canvassing, endorsing of candidates by student groups or officers, campaign spending limits, academic standing of candidates and campaign volunteers, order of names on the election ballot, dealing with complaints, and receiving and counting the votes. Voting online (by absentee ballot) or paper is possible, along with giving incentives to vote (food and drinks) at the election. The voting process (e.g., by representatives or popular vote) should be defined by the organization's bylaws.

For senate-based elections, there will be different challenges. Here the student government or organization will have a large part to play in publicizing candidates, and there are likely to be fewer election policies, especially concerning campaigning. While appropriate campaigning is important, the senators are the only ones who vote and, therefore, campaigning is directed to a limited number of students who vote on behalf of the whole student body. Campaigning may have to occur during the meeting time in order for the voting members to be informed about the candidates. Therefore, the president, when setting the agenda, should allow enough time in the meeting for campaigning and voting.

Since the senators are responsible for representing their constituents, it is recommended to have a campaigning session at the meeting prior to the election meeting. This will give the senators a chance to share candidate information with their constituents and to share the campaign brochures of the candidates, to solicit feedback on how they should vote to best represent them. Given the time constraints of a meeting, the candidates will have a limited amount of time to make their case to the senate, and it is likely that there will not be much time for questions from the floor. The amount of time will depend upon the number of positions open for election and the number of candidates vying for each position. It may also be determined, to some extent, by the amount of other business on the agenda.

If there are a large number of candidates, it is likely that there will not be a majority vote for any one of them after the first vote. In that case, a runoff election should occur between the top two candidates with the winner being decided by majority vote. One of the challenges facing student organizations is that there is sometimes a dearth of ideal candidates, and if two great candidates are vying for one position (e.g., president), then obviously, one will not be holding office the following year. It could be argued that it would be better for the health of the organization, if impressive candidates were given another opportunity to serve in an elected capacity. One way of addressing this problem is to permit candidates to run for a second position, if they are not elected for their initial position of choice. This only works if elections are done sequentially and the results are available immediately. If candidates lose the election, they can choose to enter the election for another position in a drop-down manner. Therefore, they would be permitted to make an election speech, along with the other candidates vying for that other position. One problem with the drop-down approach is that the loser of the final position that is being voted on will have no option to challenge for a second position. Of course, there are also concerns that a candidate may strategically challenge for a position earlier in the sequence, in order to get face time to help get elected for the position the student really wants. For instance, students interested in running for vice president might initially campaign for president, and if they lost that vote, they could drop down to the vice presidential election having the advantage of more visibility with the senate and two election speeches. However, the senate is usually composed of very smart students, and this strategy is likely to be transparent and could even have negative consequences. To be clear, in sequential voting paradigms, the order of voting should follow the order of offices presented in the constitution or bylaws, which beyond the president and vice president is not necessarily hierarchical.

In the case of a senate election, there should be the opportunity for the senators to state the pros and cons of a candidate. This should be time-limited and will significantly add to the time needed to be dedicated to the election process, especially if there are a large number of candidates. However, it is an important process for senators to be given the opportunity to voice their support or opposition to the rest of the voters. It is likely that those who state a pro or con will have been solicited in advance by candidates. One contentious and ethical question surrounding elections is whether the officers should overtly endorse or oppose a particular candidate. One opinion is that the officers have too much influence over the senate, and to give vocal support for a candidate either formally or informally will sway the vote, leading to unhealthy nepotism that could compromise the newly elected board and its effectiveness. The counterclaim is that officers are often best placed to judge the effectiveness or the capabilities of a candidate, especially if the candidate is a current officer; and for the benefit of the organization, it is the responsibility of the officers to make known their opinion. Other ethical issues arise when the support of an officer is being made by officers who are themselves election candidates either for a different position or running as an incumbent. Most senators, however, have a sufficient understanding of the position and the requirements necessary to serve effectively, and they are independent enough not to be swayed or fooled. Whatever the decision on this issue, it should be publicized right from the beginning of the process, to avoid any unnecessary angst and confusion and to provide grounds for addressing any unethical behavior that may arise.

Once the new board has been elected, they should be formally presented to the school community through the student organization's Web site and, if possible, the student newspaper. It is also the responsibility of the outgoing president to notify the school administrators of the new leadership with whom they will be dealing in the coming year. This can be done by a letter with the names and a brief bio and photograph of each candidate and their position on the board or by directing the administrators to the student organization's Web site, where a photograph of the whole new board could be displayed on the front page.

## Transition Meetings

Once the new board has been elected, the outgoing president's last responsibility, in most cases, is to transition from the old to the new leadership. This may take the form of a daylong retreat or at least an extended period of time that can be devoted to building the new team and orienting them to the history, relationships, and advocacy that are ongoing. Transition meetings could begin with food and should follow the order of getting to know each other, the organization, and the vision for the next year in office.

### Getting to know each other

If time is limited, members should at least introduce themselves by pronouncing their full name, field of study, and background. Ideally, the president would have some icebreakers in order to help the new and old teams bond. An example of one that works well is where the president would ask each member of the old and new teams to share something bizarre about themselves, in secret to the president about a week before the meeting. Such examples may include the following: "I've driven a train"; "I've been on reality TV"; "I speak four languages"; etc. The president would then create a list of these bizarre talents or experiences on a sheet of paper, and at the meeting each person would be given a copy of the sheet and try to find out which team member was associated with which bizarre experience or talent. This should be timed and the person who matches up the most correctly wins a prize. This icebreaker gets people moving and talking, and in a very short time, members know something strange about their colleagues. Another possible idea is to get a list of about twenty scrambled words, say names of cars, flowers, or vegetables, and the new officers are paired up with their outgoing counterparts to figure them all out before the other teams to win a prize. This gets the transitioning officers working together in advance of their formal transition later in the meeting. Finally, the most competitive icebreaker should be reserved for the outgoing team to challenge the incoming leadership team. One example might be to ask each team to create a one minute radio commercial for the organization and a new logo, both of which must be shared with the whole group at the end of the task. This could take about 20 minutes and, as can be imagined, the new team would likely approach this much more seriously than the outgoing team. This icebreaker gets the new team focusing together on a project in a competitive environment, trying to outdo their outgoing colleagues. It is worthwhile investing in a book of icebreakers and teambuilding games for occasions such as transition meetings or retreats.

### Getting to know the organization

The next part of the meeting should be an orientation to the organization. It should consist of two parts: A general overview of the organization and the school/department, so that all the new officers can have an understanding of the political framework within which they are about to function; and secondly, a specific orientation to the officers' positional responsibilities. The general overview should focus on the structure of the organization, its history, accomplishments, place within the school/department, the school/department administrative structure and leadership, the relationships that have been developed with administrators, and finally the ongoing advocacy and initiatives that may not have been fully completed the previous year. You may want to have an organizational chart of the senior administration, showing which position oversees what area, who reports to whom within each area, and the key decision makers and those who have worked closely with your group.

The second part of this familiarization process should be much more specific, and each outgoing officer should spend considerable time and care orienting the new officer to the specific responsibilities of the position. This specific orientation will differ depending on the individual and position. However, some basic rules should apply to each pairing. The outgoing officers should share their initial vision and expectations and whether they were met or not. They should also share how they fulfilled the expectations of their position, at least one success and one failure, and any ongoing or unfinished advocacy. The incoming officers should be free to ask questions of the outgoing officers and share their vision for the position and their reasons for seeking election.

### Getting to know the new vision

After the officer orientations, both teams could come together for some food/drinks and a final bidding of best wishes, whereupon the role of the outgoing team will be finished. The rest of the retreat is for the new board only, as they meet to share their individual visions with each other and hear the organizational vision from the incoming president. This can be an interesting time, especially if the vision of the president is different from the visions of some of the individually elected officers. It is best to set all the visions on the table and openly share them with the other officers, with the understanding that things will probably change by the time the new term begins. Where differences arise, the president should meet individually with the officers at another time to meld their goals. It is worth remembering that since each officer has been elected, the president cannot fire officers for having and pursuing different goals, especially if the officers were elected having made their goals known. In most cases, differences are small and can easily be accommodated into an overarching common goal of unified representation of the student body. Unity is extremely important and the onus is on the president to harness the differences and unite the new officers in their passion for student well-being to form a harmonious group. Depending on the leadership style of the president and on the personalities of the individuals this can take time, but time spent in this pursuit is productive. The joy of service can quickly be drained, due to an acrimonious board that spends more time fighting with each other rather than focusing on their elected responsibilities. Much of the time of the president and vice presidents can be wasted if attention is not paid early enough to unifying the group through teambuilding and, in some cases, compromise. The student body and the administrators with whom the leaders of the organization work are much more likely to respect a unified and productive board than a divisive and ineffective one.

## Training New Officers

The effectiveness of the organization depends to some extent on the training and integration of the new officers into the school community. This is a very important role of the outgoing officers and, if possible, the new board should be in place before the end of the school term, so that the outgoing officers can personally introduce their replacements to the appropriate students and administrators. It may be the privilege of an officer to have a seat on some very important school committees. If the election has occurred in time, the outgoing officer should ask the administrative chairs of the school committees on which they serve if they can formally introduce their replacement at the final meeting of the year. This will usually be accommodated and the new board member can expect to stay for part or even for all of the meeting. Similarly, any student committees that the outgoing officer chairs should be introduced to the new officer who would, presumably, be expected to assume the chair's role the following year. It is also possible that the outgoing officers could invite administrators, with whom they have worked closely, for coffee where they could less formally introduce them to the incoming board member, presuming the working relationship would be continuous.

For elected officers who are new to the organization or board, it is important to have them attend a board meeting, where they can observe and even contribute to the issues being discussed. Of course, they would not be permitted to vote on issues until the first meeting of the new academic year. However, they could make meaningful contributions and observations that would help with a smooth transition into the position and a seamless transition of leadership.

## Documenting Officers' Roles

A big problem for many student organizations is inadequate transitioning, especially because student groups can have high turnover with loss of critical information from people who graduate or leave. It is important that the outgoing officers thoroughly document what they do for the organization for their successor, as if the new officer had to take over immediately without the opportunity to go through a normal transition.

Electronic files should be saved to your organization's account and backed up regularly providing a historical resource for future officers.

## Officer and Committee Reports

Many responsible organizations will have a mid-year and/or an end-of-year report outlining the vision and the accomplishments to the constituents and to the school administration. This demonstrates transparency and accountability to all stakeholders and, if the report is presented well, demonstrates professionalism. This is a real opportunity to showcase the organization to the world (if the report is to be posted on the Web), and since there will be many interested parties, it is an opportunity to earn respect from people you don't even know directly. You would be surprised by how many successful alumni were involved in leadership roles in student organizations, and their interest never seems to leave them. Many alumni will be looking to see how the student organization is represented and what advocacy is either new or ongoing. Some even go as far as to make contact with officers who serve in positions that they once held to offer their support or just to see how things have changed. As a student leader, there may be tremendous opportunities to meet important alumni and trustees, all of whom have a great deal of concern for student life. Then, you can present them with a high quality publication filled with remarkable achievements to make a great and lasting impression. There is also a legacy factor in student organizations, and the best and worst student leaders are remembered by the administration and students for years to come. It behooves your organization immensely to have strong leadership and to build upon a strong legacy, especially where great relationships have developed and respect has been earned.

The mid-year and end-of-year reports are similar documents, with the mid-year report being somewhat prospective and the end-of-year report reflecting on the year's accomplishments. The president should write a general introduction to the organization, the mission statement, and the strategic plan the officers had for their year in office. This should be followed by a detailed breakdown of the finances and structure of the organization, so that those reading it can easily and quickly understand the group and its budget. Since the budget and organizational structure are usually determined among the board, senate, and/or school administration, it is not always transparent to others exactly how student leadership is organized. The mid- and end-of-year reports are a valuable medium for sharing this information. After the finances and organizational structure, there should be a summary by the president of all the accomplishments, the issues on the table for advocacy, and the number of students positively engaged or affected by the existence of the group. In order to make sure that all elected officers have the chance to contribute to the report and justify their position to those who elected them, it is recommended to have a page dedicated to each position on the board with half of a page for each committee chair. Encourage the officers and committee chairs to treat this as a celebration of their achievements, and inform them that this is an opportunity to make a great impression on the readers. These pages could include photographs of the officer and a very brief academic bio, such as years in the program, degree sought, and expected graduation date. Then, they can share their accomplishments and any progress on unfinished business they are leaving for their successor.

It is also advisable to invite the school administrators who have been assigned to oversee student organizations and with whom you have probably worked quite closely, to contribute to your report. They will probably appreciate the opportunity to be featured in such a formal and high profile report, and they will most likely have something great to say about you and your organization. A simple courtesy invitation will be a win-win situation all around.

Since you are going to be sending this report to just about every relevant person including the school's president, chancellor, dean, or principal, the most important section at the end of the report is the acknowledgements. Do not spend any time thinking about who you would leave out. Make sure that every school administrator or trustee who has helped you in any way is listed in the acknowledgements section. Once school administrators see that there is an acknowledgements section listed in the Table of Contents, you can be sure, they will be looking for their name, and rightly so. Therefore, in all seriousness, don't leave anyone off the list who deserves to be mentioned! When the student body sees the long list of people you are acknowledging, they will also be impressed, given that you have been elected to represent their issues to the school's leadership. Of course, saying "thank you" in public is one of the best strategies you can employ as a student leader. The thing to remember especially about the end-of-year report is that the report is a document of record, which is going to be kept by the school administration and your organization as part of the history and legacy of your group. If it is well presented, it will probably be referred to long after you have left office when a student or an administrator is looking for information on your organization. It is time, money, and effort well spent to produce a spectacular report.

## Recognizing Achievements

While it is very important to acknowledge the assistance of school administration and other partners in your successful year as a student

leader, it is more important to recognize the hard work, time sacrificed, and dedication of those members of the student body, senate, or board who have been integral to the organization's success. Most of the individuals will be volunteers who have not been remunerated for their efforts but who have worked out of a passion for a particular issue, organization, or the student body in general. It is an acceptable use of your budget to have an end-of-year awards ceremony, for purposes of recognizing those students who have contributed to the success of your organization during the year. There can be an arrangement of prizes and awards ranging from nicely printed and signed certificates of appreciation to engraved plaques, depending on the level of award or budget. It is highly appropriate to celebrate a year of hard work and accomplishment, and to say "thank you" to those who have worked alongside you is worth more than you will probably ever know. As with the acknowledgements section of the end-of-year report, do not spend any time thinking about who should not be getting an award. Everyone serving your organization should be getting, at least, a certificate of appreciation or other form of recognition. Where possible, the awardees should be chosen in partnership with the representatives of the student body, such as the senate. There may be certain prestigious annual awards consisting of the following: senator of the year, committee of the year, student organization of the year, volunteer of the year, board member of the year, service award, etc. Having the senate nominate and even vote on the recipients is appropriate for a leader to do and removes any notion of nepotism or impression that the recipients may not be truly representative. Depending upon the available budget, the recognition could take the form of a banquet with a nicely printed program for each guest, a simple appetizer-type food buffet, or even pizza. However it is planned, it should be a celebration of the great year that has passed while rewarding those who contributed. It is also well-founded public relations to invite administrators and alumni who have been involved with the organization during the year to the awards ceremony and, if appropriate, to include them among the award recipients, though the focus should be on awarding students for their work.

If you have budgeted for a fancy reception or banquet, you should try to go all out and make it as impressive as funds will allow. Nice invitations should be sent out well in advance with RSVP expected by a certain date, so that the right number of meal plates can be ordered. The event may be either held on campus or in a local restaurant, but it is recommended to support the school's catering/food services if it has a suitable venue and menu. You should consider having a period of gathering and appetizers/drinks for about thirty minutes prior to the start of the meal. This will allow students to socialize and find their table,

while permitting the hosts, presumably the officers, to meet and greet the guests. If there is a music department at your institution, it would add a pleasing touch to have a quartet playing during the reception and even during the meal. Seating can either be open or, if you have asked for RSVPs, arranged. Such gatherings are great opportunities for students to mingle and network, especially given the somewhat isolated nature of some programs where interdisciplinary study is uncommon. At the appointed time, the president of the organization should invite guests to take their seats and formally open the ceremony with a few words of welcome and an invitation to begin eating. In student gatherings, it is fun to show a multimedia presentation of the past year, with music, photographs, and even video. This might be the last responsibility of the public relations officer/committee: prepare a multimedia presentation of the student organization for the guests at the awards ceremony. '

It may be that there is a guest speaker or each of the major awardees is invited to speak for a couple of minutes. The president should begin the formal award portion of the ceremony by making some remarks about the year, perhaps in tandem with a multimedia presentation. Do not be shy during this presentation. If the aim is to celebrate achievements, then include even the smallest accomplishments and any advocacy that is in progress. Advocating for changes in school policy is a lengthy process, with achievements sometimes taking more than an academic year, demonstrating the importance of a great transition between leadership and a sustained and coordinated advocacy platform. Therefore, it is highly appropriate to include as an achievement the opening of discourse about an issue that will have to be closed by the incoming student leadership. After the awards have been presented, the finale should be the presentation and brief introduction of the newly elected officers with closing remarks and a charge to look forward to the next year from the incoming president. This would mark the formal transition of leadership and new vision for the student organization.

# Chapter 10

# How to Improve or Turn Around a Student Organization

## Overview of the Improvement Process

Organizations will inevitably encounter numerous problems and challenges. The failure to address issues as soon as they arise can have a devastating effect, potentially leading to the demise of your organization. To help solve organizational problems, a seven step process is presented in Figure 10. To continuously improve the organization, the process should be repeated for every new problem or challenge encountered and a committee may be formed to address the concerns.

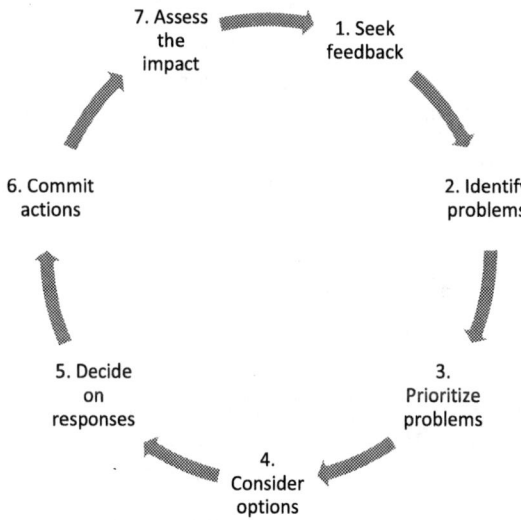

**Figure 10: Improvement Cycle**

### 1. Seek feedback

Often, not all of your organization's problems will be known to you. As a result, you will need to actively and continuously seek feedback from others to identify issues before they grow to become more difficult to solve. One way to get feedback on your organization is through an evaluation checklist such as the one in Table 10.

## Table 10: Organization Checklist

| Factor | Attributes | Rating | Comments |
|---|---|---|---|
| Accomplishments | Addressing Issues and Concerns | | |
| Advising | Availability and Involvement | | |
| Advertising | Promotional Items and Materials | | |
| Advocacy | Success with Administrators | | |
| Board | Chair and Board Members | | |
| Budget | Money Available and Spent | | |
| Committees | Chairs and Activities | | |
| Communication | Effectiveness and Technologies | | |
| Elections | Candidates and Successors | | |
| Equipment | Computers, Printers, and Copiers | | |
| Expenditures | Food, Drinks, and Supplies | | |
| Meetings | Attendance, Frequency, and Efficiency | | |
| Membership | Number of Active Members | | |
| Morale | Among Board/Committee Members | | |
| Office | Availability, Adequacy, and Furniture | | |
| Programs | Number, Turnout, and Satisfaction | | |
| Recruitment | Filling Open Positions | | |
| Reputation | Among Administrators and Members | | |
| Satisfaction | Among Board and Members | | |
| Staff | Adequacy and Productivity | | |
| Storage Space | Availability and Adequacy | | |
| Structure | Constitution and Bylaws | | |
| Support | Funding and Staffing | | |
| Training | For Board Members and Successors | | |
| Turnover rate | Retention and Loss Rates | | |
| Web site | Complete, Error-free, and Up-to-date | | |

The rating can be Satisfactory/Unsatisfactory/Neutral (represented by S/U/N) or a numerical scale (e.g., 1-5). Both the Factors and Attributes may be customized for your particular organization. The Comments column could contain any important notes or explanations associated with the rating of a given factor.

An online form could also be posted on your organization's Web site that allows members to submit feedback and suggestions that would help your group. To reach a broader audience your organization can use an online survey tool to help design, conduct, and analyze a survey of all members. To identify problems within your board, you can administer a survey for all of your board members. Such surveys offer members anonymity and time to carefully think about how they might respond. Examples of these kinds of surveys can be found in the Appendix.

Nevertheless, for any problems in your organization, you should try to create a culture that encourages others to let you know of issues as soon as they arise. The feedback should come from a variety of sources including your board, members, staff, advisor, and alumni. Meeting with your advisor and board specifically to review your organization is helpful. The need for open communication is critical.

## 2. Identify problems

From Table 10, the counts and/or averages of the ratings may be calculated for each factor and sorted by their rating as a way to prioritize the issues. Examining those factors that had the worst ratings should help to identify problems and their possible sources, in addition to examining frequently identified problems even if they are small. A spreadsheet listing all of the problems can be created and presented to the board and/or committee charged with addressing the issues.

## 3. Prioritize problems

Once you have a list of the problems, you should not expect to solve them all at once. As the leader, you will need to prioritize the problems and focus on the most critical ones first before addressing the rest of them. Sometimes it is necessary to solve those frequently occurring, albeit possibly small, problems first.

A severity scheme may also be devised to rank the problems. For example, on a severity scale ranging from 1 to 5, those with severity level of 5 would cause more damage to the organization than one with a severity level of 1. For instance, problems with a budgetary impact on your organization could be assigned severity levels based on financial costs associated with them: the higher the cost, the higher the severity level that would be assigned to them. Your board or the appropriate committee should agree on the priority assigned to the issues.

## 4. Consider options

For all problems, your team should look at every possible option to solve them. Moving ahead with only one option without considering others can be risky. You will also need to consider the impact of your decisions and the consequences of your actions, making sure that you do not create new problems while trying to solve existing ones. If you and your team have trouble determining a possible solution for any given problem, you should ask your advisor and/or other student organization advisement staff at your school. Be certain that none of your choices would violate any school policies; any of them that do must be eliminated.

5. **Decide on responses**

Once you have considered all of your options, you will need to decide on a response strategy. Cost may be a consideration for weighing alternative responses, as might complexity, feasibility, probability of success, and resources needed. In many cases, your board would be expected to approve the responses. A series of backup plans should be devised in case the actions taken to solve the problems do not work so that if plan A fails, plan B or C can be carried out. Even backup plans for backup plans are helpful!

6. **Commit actions**

Once you have decided on the best response, you will need to follow through on executing your strategy. Be prepared to execute back-up plans for failures and worst-case scenarios. An exemplary leader is receptive of criticism from others, particularly from those who care about the organization. A leader who is too defensive will discourage members from pointing out future problems. Turning the mistakes into learning experiences and turning problems into opportunities will make your organization better. Implementing major changes gradually can also help, and in turn, the effects of any change will be easier to isolate and measure for effectiveness.

7. **Assess the impact**

After you have committed actions to solve problems, you will need to assess their impact to consider whether the problems have been actually solved. Measures of success could include cost savings, increased participation in previously under-attended programs, or general agreement from members that the problem has been resolved. Consider recording the resolution of issues in your organization's archives to serve as a historical record for future leaders. This can be recorded in a database or in a repository of files on computers that are backed up regularly. As a result of the evaluation and appropriate action, changes may be required to the bylaws or constitution and such changes will need to be approved by the majority of the board members.

## Forming a Task Force

To perform process improvement, you may want to designate members of your organization to form a task force, also known as an ad hoc committee. Such a group would be tasked with the responsibility of finding ways to make your organization better. Members outside of your group and possible inclusion of former board members including alumni can help in removing biases and resistance to new ways of thinking. Recruiting members outside of your board who have had a successful record as student leaders or who have given valuable feedback on surveys can be helpful. You may even be able to recruit them to serve on your board to help your organization even more!

## Improving Morale and Performance

Teamwork is essential in student organizations, and maintaining a successful working relationship with high morale is of great concern to a student leader. It is important that your team feels appreciated by you. Regular positive feedback can help create a culture of hard work and transmit a positive vibe within the organization's leadership that will spread throughout the membership. As the leader, you need to take the initiative in creating an affirming and nurturing climate, especially after an organization evaluation where difficult problems and challenges need to be addressed resulting in changes to the group. Scheduling events for board and/or committee members to celebrate birthdays, playing board, video or sporting games, holding a dinner, luncheon, retreat or scavenger hunt, etc. are all great ways to maintain a positive team. All such efforts at appreciation and teambuilding will be appreciated by those concerned.

Student governments in some of the bigger schools are able to pay a small stipend to board members or committee chairs. However, most student organizations would not be able to afford to pay people for such work. Therefore, incentive strategies such as monthly/yearly awards for outstanding performance are commonly employed to reward staff, board members, senators, committees, regular members, committee chairs, and organizations. Having such incentives encourages people to do a better job and rewards those who have done exceptional work serving as examples for others.

## Demoting vs. Dismissing Board Members

One of the most difficult tasks for any leader is reorganization of the leadership team or structure that involves the demotion or dismissal of individuals from their posts. Unproductive or unethical individuals do not belong in your team and could cause significant damage to the reputation of your organization.

Demoting and reassigning a board member is possible in certain cases, and such procedures should be clearly defined in your constitution or bylaws. Sometimes a particular position of responsibility can be too much for specific board members, and they may be reassigned to another role such as a committee chair, where they can still help out without as much responsibility. At times, there are some board members who violate your organization's constitution or bylaws, or they are simply causing trouble or not performing their duties. Reassigning such individuals may just be reassigning the misery. Board members who fail to perform their responsibilities set a bad example, create more work for others, and make your life more stressful. In such times you could be faced with the decision of whether or not you should dismiss a board member. It is wise to follow a process of warning and retraining before dismissing.

You should first warn them verbally and in writing via e-mail clearly outlining the reason for the warning, indicating necessary actions to redress the situation or face possible removal from office. If possible, give them three warnings just like in a ball game (three strikes and you're out), making references to your organization's constitution or bylaws. Sending a written warning helps avoid a challenge to having been warned and indicates the seriousness with which you aim to address the behavior. Facilitating a change in attitude or behavior is the ideal outcome of such a warning. However, some people refuse to change and if this is the case, you should seek to replace the board member by following the procedures for removal and replacement in line with your constitution or bylaws. When leaders engage in the warning and removal process, a clear message is sent to the membership demonstrating the seriousness with which they regard their office and the responsibility they have to ensure a healthy organization.

## Resigning from Office

It is possible that a situation arises where you are no longer able to remain as the leader of an organization. Perhaps there has been a death, serious injury, or illness in your family or other unforeseen circumstances that make being a successful leader nearly impossible for you. In such cases, it might be in the best interest of the organization for you to resign. In line with your constitution or bylaws, a successor should be selected and you should make every effort to ensure a smooth transition of leadership, especially if the new leader is not from within your board or leadership team.

## Running a Special Election

To fill up openings as a result of possible resignations or dismissals of board members including yourself, you may consider running a special election to fill positions until the end of the academic year. Remember to be careful with the timing, so that you are not running such an election around the finals week. In such a case, waiting until the beginning of the next term would be advised whenever possible.

Chapter 9 covers material regarding elections and transitions. The election needs to be conducted in line with your constitution and bylaws. After the election is held, remember to aim for a smooth transition by allowing adequate time for newly elected members to ramp up to speed on their responsibilities.

## Restructuring an Organization

There may be problems with the way your organization is structured. Perhaps there are not enough positions, or the responsibilities may not be properly defined or fairly distributed. To solve this problem, you should review your constitution and bylaws. The descriptions for the positions may need to be updated with responsibilities rearranged to distribute the workload evenly, so that no one gets burned out.

New positions and committees can be added to help with certain functions that prove too hard to be carried by the existing board. The titles for positions and committees can be updated to more adequately reflect the current needs of your organization.

Examine how your organization functions and seek ways to improve your group's processes on a continuous basis. The bylaws describing how your organization operates may need to be updated. Figure 3 from Chapter 3 shows the steps and process to follow when updating your constitution and bylaws.

## Transforming an Organization

There may be a time when an organization faces the possibility of being shut down or being placed on probation by the institution or other governing body. If you are running a student chapter, for instance, many national organizations require a certain number of members in order to gain or retain recognition status. If previous leadership has violated institutional policies, your institution may place sanctions on your organization, even though you may not have been involved with the infraction. In such a case, your role as a leader is to regain the trust of the institutional leadership, through prompt attention to the issues and perhaps through restructuring of the organization.

You can make your organization better by studying other successful groups and by partnering with a related one. Two groups could even merge and create a synergistic effect helping form a better organization than either one. The name of your group may need to be changed to adequately reflect the resulting organization. Any major transformations of your organization should be carefully considered in light of your constitution and bylaws and in consultation with your advisor. Such sweeping changes must win the approval of a majority of the board members and, whenever possible, a majority of the members before being adopted.

## Changing the Advisor

There may be times when it becomes necessary to change your advisor. Examples of such situations include an advisor who is leaving the institution or advancing to a different position making them unable to serve as an advisor anymore; or more disturbingly, an advisor who is inattentive or offers consistently bad advice.

Before changing advisors, you should approach them to find out whether they are able to meet your expectations or needs, especially if you are a new leader and just beginning your relationship with them. If they continue to be ineffective or decide that they are unable to make the necessary commitment, you and your board should begin the process of appointing a new advisor. If at all possible, try to make the transition as easy as possible, maintaining a decent relationship with the outgoing advisor. It is important that you act with integrity and respect towards the outgoing and incoming advisors, who may be colleagues and whose affiliation with the organization and each other should be amicable. The board should approve of the new advisor, and the membership should be informed.

Every leader should be concerned about the health of the organization and should be continually focused on evaluation and improvement. Complacency will lead to the demise of the organization and in the student setting, where leadership necessarily changes fairly frequently, it is essential that no leader rest on the laurels of the previous leadership. A student organization needs to maintain momentum through ambitious and dedicated leaders every year. Change for change sake is not a cure-all, but occasionally an overhaul is needed. If the interests of the organization and respect for all individuals concerned are foremost, the fall-out will be minimal and the turnaround of a poorly functioning group will be more successful.

## Conclusion

In this chapter, we have proposed ideas and approaches we found to be successful in improving student organizations we have led and others we have advised or consulted. This book is intended to serve as a guide in assisting you with the responsibilities, challenges, and privileges of student leadership. We hope that you find it helpful in making you a better student leader, and we hope that your organization consequently improves. Sincerely, we invite you to let us know whether reading this guide has had any impact upon you or your organization. Hence, please feel welcome to visit our Web site at **www.studentorgleader.com** anytime and submit the contact form with your feedback.

Ultimately, we wish you all the best of success as a student leader in your organization!

# Appendix A: Sample Constitution

## CONSTITUTION OF THE
## CHAPTER OF THE

_____

### ARTICLE I – ORGANIZATION

#### Section 1 – Name
This organization shall be known as the Chapter, hereinafter called the "Chapter" of _____, hereafter referred to as *ACRONYM*.

#### Section 2 – Purpose
The objective of the Chapter is to promote the profession of _____ through the organized effort of this group in study, research, and discussion of the field of _____ and the dissemination of knowledge thereby gained. The Chapter shall promote membership in *ACRONYM* by acquainting the student body with the ideas, purposes, and objectives of *ACRONYM*.

#### Section 3 – Membership
Any student or alumnus of the School who also holds membership with *ACRONYM* is eligible for membership in the Chapter.

### ARTICLE II – BOARD MEMBERS

#### Section 1 – President
A. Duties and Responsibilities
   1. Oversee all Chapter activities.
   2. Organize and conduct regular meetings with all Board members.
   3. Meet with the Chapter's Advisor regularly to address concerns of the Chapter.
B. Vacancy
   If the position of President is vacant, the Executive Vice President shall become President.

#### Section 2 – Executive Vice President
A. Duties and Responsibilities
   1. Recruit any available positions of officers and directors for the Chapter.
   2. Coordinate with any other people or organizations in conjunction with Chapter activities.
   3. Serve as the liaison with academia, alumni, and industry.
B. Vacancy

If the position of Executive Vice President is vacant, another Officer, Director, Committee Chair, or Chapter Member shall be appointed to the vacant position by a majority vote of the Officers.

## Section 3 – Vice President of Finance
A. Duties and Responsibilities
1. Prepare a budget for each Chapter activity.
2. Maintain records of all the Chapter's expenditures.
3. Handle purchasing for the Chapter's activities.
B. Vacancy
If the position of Vice President of Finance is vacant, another Officer, Director, Committee Chair, or Chapter Member shall be appointed to the vacant position by a majority vote of the Officers.

## Section 4 – Vice President of Programming
A. Duties and Responsibilities
1. Support the planning, organizing, and execution of Chapter events and activities.
2. Reserve rooms for Chapter events and meetings.
3. Coordinate with any other people or organizations in conjunction with Chapter activities.
B. Vacancy
If the position of Vice President of Programming is vacant, another Officer, Director, Committee Chair, or Chapter Member shall be appointed to the vacant position by a majority vote of the Officers.

## Section 5 – Vice President of Communications
A. Duties and Responsibilities
1. Send mail and e-mail correspondence of the Chapter.
2. Maintain the approved Constitution and any Bylaws of the Chapter.
3. Take minutes for all meetings to be approved at the following Board meeting.
B. Vacancy
If the position of Vice President of Communications is vacant, another Officer, Director, Committee Chair, or Chapter Member shall be appointed to the vacant position by a majority vote of the Officers.

## Section 6 – Vice President of Publicity
A. Duties and Responsibilities
1. Maintain the Chapter's Web site.
2. Design and post flyers for the Chapter's events.
3. Advertise and promote the Chapter's events.
B. Vacancy

If the position of Vice President of Publicity is vacant, another Officer, Director, Committee Chair, or Chapter Member shall be appointed to the vacant position by a majority vote of the Officers.

## Section 7 – Vice President of Membership
A. Duties and Responsibilities
   1. Recruit members to join the Chapter.
   2. Receive and process membership applications received and send to the *ACRONYM* national office.
   3. Keep track of all the names and e-mail addresses of all Chapter members.
B. Vacancy

   If the position of Vice President of Membership is vacant, another Officer, Director, Committee Chair, or Chapter Member shall be appointed to the vacant position by a majority vote of the Officers.

## Section 8 – Directors and Committee Chairs
A. The Chapter may establish Directors and/or Chairs for Committees and nominate Chapter members to serve as Directors or Committee Chairs by a majority vote of the Officers.
B. If the position as Director or Committee Chair is vacant, another Chapter Member shall be appointed to the vacant position by a majority vote of the Officers.


## ARTICLE III – ELIGIBILITY, TERMS, AND REMOVAL

### Section 1 – Eligibility Requirements
All members must be enrolled as School students to be eligible for any Chapter position of office.

### Section 2 – Terms of Office
All Officers, Directors, and Committee Chairs serve a term of one year, beginning from the day after graduation of the current year to graduation day in the following year.

### Section 3 – Removal from Office
Any Officers, Directors, and Committee Chairs may be removed from office by a vote of at least three-fourths of the Officers upon receiving advanced notification, in cases where the officer consistently fails to perform the required duties of that position without a justifiable reason.

## ARTICLE IV – AMENDMENTS

Amendments to this Constitution are to be submitted in writing before approval. To become effective, amendments must be approved by at least three-fourths of the Officers.

## ARTICLE V – AFFILIATIONS

### Section 1 – Recognition

The Chapter is a recognized student organization at the School, but is not a part of the School itself.

### Section 2 – Referral

In all correspondence and business transactions, the Chapter may refer to itself as an organization at the School but not as part of the School itself.

### Section 3 – Responsibilities

The Chapter accepts full financial and production responsibility for all activities it sponsors.

### Section 4 – Policies and Regulations

The Chapter agrees to abide by all pertinent School policies and regulations. Where School policies and regulations and those of *ACRONYM* differ, the policies and regulations of the School will take precedence.

### Section 5 – Legal Liability

The Chapter recognizes and understands that the School assumes no legal liability for the actions of the organization, and that the School is not providing blanket indemnification insurance coverage for any activities of the organization, unless those activities expressly benefit and further the goals of the School and have received prior review, approval, and consent of the Offices of Student Affairs, Risk Management, and/or General Counsel.

# Appendix B: Sample Bylaws

## BYLAWS OF THE

_____

## I.  PROTOCOLS .

### A. Senate Meeting Protocols

1. *ACRONYM* should normally have Senate meetings twice a month during the academic year at times when most Senators can attend.

2. Notifications for meetings should be sent out at least one week in advance of the meeting to all Senators. Notifications should include the time, date, and location of the meeting. A reminder should be sent out about 24 hours in advance of the meeting to the Senators.

3. Reservation of a room should be made at least one week in advance of a Senate meeting.

4. Meetings should be conducted using Parliamentary Procedures.

5. Meeting minutes are to be read and approved at the following Senate meeting. Minutes should contain a list of the Senators in attendance, the items discussed, and decisions made.

6. Senators are expected to arrive on time to each meeting and to remain until the conclusion of the meeting.

7. Matters concerning visitors should occur at the beginning of the meetings. After such matters have been addressed, the visitors are to be dismissed for the remainder of the meeting.

8. Funding proposals with dollar amounts and debate should occur in the absence of the visitors for which the funding applies. Once a decision has been reached by the Senate regarding the funding, those requesting funding may be notified of the results afterwards.

9. Candidates for unfilled posts should address the Senate before a vote. When there is more than one candidate for an unfilled position, voting by secret ballot should be conducted with a Senator collecting the votes and counting them under the supervision of another Senator.

10. A status report should be delivered orally by each Senator detailing any accomplishments, activities, issues, plans, problems, and suggestions arising since the last Senate meeting.

11. Senators should give others the chance to speak and should not interrupt speakers.
12. No personal attacks or offensive remarks should be made during a Senate meeting.

B. **General Meeting Protocols**

1. *ACRONYM* should have at least one General Meeting in the fall term and at least one in the spring term, in addition to the Election Meeting.
2. The Senators should agree on a time for each General Meeting at which most Senators can attend.
3. Reservation of a room should be made at least two weeks in advance of a General Meeting to ensure availability.
4. An agenda should be established at least one week in advance outlining the topics to be presented by each member designated to present.
5. Initial advertisement should take place at least one week in advance prior to the day of the General Meeting.
6. All Senators should be present at the General Meeting, arriving prior to the scheduled time and staying until the conclusion of the General Meeting.
7. Each Senator should speak at some point during each General Meeting.

C. **E-mail Protocols**

1. Senators should check their e-mail at least once a day during the weekdays.
2. Personal attacks or offensive remarks should not be contained in e-mail sent to Senators from other Senators.
3. All e-mail should include a relevant subject line to make tracking previous messages easier.
4. All e-mail should be checked for spelling and grammar before being sent.
5. All e-mail should contain accurate information. If mistakes are made, then e-mail should be resent with corrections.
6. Replying to all recipients or replying by e-mail to more than just the sender should be reserved to times when recipients need to be informed of the response.
7. Senators should send e-mail to specific/all Senators and/or the Advisor when such recipients need to be informed of the e-mail. Senators should use careful judgment when sending or forwarding e-mail to others by only selecting recipients who need to be informed of the e-mail.

## II. PROCEDURES

### A. Procedures for *ACRONYM* Activities

1. The date and funding for an event should be approved by the Senate well in advance of the event.
2. Any purchase orders and funding requests from the student government should be made by the appropriate deadlines to be approved.
3. An advertisement for an event/sign-up should be distributed to all student departmental mailing lists by the department representatives at least one week in advance of a proposed event/sign-up and posted on the *ACRONYM* Web site as soon as possible. A reminder should be sent out about 24 hours before the actual event/sign-up.
4. A staff plan for the sign-up/setup/execution/wrap-up/ticket distribution should be drawn up with each participating Senator's knowledge and consent.
5. The participating Senators are expected to arrive on time and complete their required tasks during the assigned time.
6. Students who sign up must show their school ID card, and the student's name, department, and school ID number are to be recorded on a sign-up sheet by the assigned Senator.
7. When any tickets have been received, the ticket distribution information should be posted on the *ACRONYM* Web site.

### B. Election Procedures

1. These Election Procedures are to be completed during the spring term by April 30 each year.
2. An Election Committee of at least three Senators and/or Members who are not candidates in the Election should be formed to run the Election, based on approval from the Senate.
3. A Notice is to be sent out via e-mail to the Members and posted on the *ACRONYM* Web site at least one week in advance of a filing deadline.
4. This Notice will list all *ACRONYM* positions for the next academic year and include references to the responsibilities listed for each position in the Constitution at the *ACRONYM* Web site.
5. The Notice must state the Eligibility Requirements for any *ACRONYM* position as follows:
   a) A candidate must be currently enrolled as a student in our school.

b) A candidate must be enrolled as a student in our school for the fall term of the current year.

c) A candidate for a department representative position must be a student from the same department to be considered as a candidate in the election.

6. The Notice shall state that candidates must reply via e-mail to _____ by a given deadline supplying their complete student name, student ID number, and the position being sought.

7. Once a candidate has been cleared for eligibility, a Confirmation will be sent via e-mail from the *ACRONYM* account to the candidate, confirming the time and date of the election with the candidate's desired position listed in the body of the message.

8. After all confirmations have been sent out, an Announcement of the Election containing the date, time, and location of the General Meeting will be sent out to the Members via e-mail.

9. During this General Meeting where the Election will be held, ballots for those positions having more than one candidate with the candidates' names and corresponding positions will be distributed to all of the members attending.

10. The candidates for each Senate position should be introduced by a member of the Election Committee.

11. Each candidate will be allowed a chance to speak briefly and answer a limited number of questions from the Members present, while the competing candidates are not in the room.

12. For uncontested positions, the candidate is expected to face away from the audience while a vote by raising hands is conducted. For department representatives, only those members may vote for the members of their own department.

13. Ballots are only necessary for contested positions. The ballots must contain a spot for the voter's name, department, and username, which must be filled out completely for the ballot to count.

14. Each Member's vote is to be kept secret and never to be disclosed.

15. Only students currently enrolled at the _____ are allowed to vote in this Election, and only one ballot is allowed for each Member voting.

16. Members are only allowed to vote for the department representative of their own department.

17. Ballots should be collected, verified, and counted by the Election Committee as soon as possible with any ties resolved by the Senate.

18. For any Senate position, the candidate with the most number of votes wins.
19. If there are any remaining open positions, these must be filled by the successors of the current Senate.
20. If any position becomes open at any time during the entire successive academic year, any remaining eligible candidates who had run in the election but had not been elected to a Senate position may be nominated to fill an open position.
21. The successive Senate must approve the candidates for any position to be filled after the Election, based on majority vote.

## III. POLICIES

### A. Ticket Distribution

1. Members who sign up for an *ACRONYM* ticket are required to present a valid school ID card and pay the required amount in cash during the sign-up time.
2. *ACRONYM* generally distributes only one ticket for each student during the ticket distribution for an activity.
3. Members are expected to claim any tickets for which they have signed up by presenting a valid school ID card, during the times and place in which such tickets are distributed. *ACRONYM* is not responsible for distributing unclaimed tickets.
4. *ACRONYM* is not expected to refund money for any tickets sold.

### B. Participation

1. *ACRONYM* activities are for students only, but may on occasion be extended to include faculty and staff.
2. Eligibility for participation in *ACRONYM* activities will be routinely verified by Senators.

### C. E-mail

1. Only official *ACRONYM* e-mail should be sent to the department distribution lists of students for the departments. Non-official *ACRONYM* messages may be sent to the _____ newsgroup.
2. Those members of such departmental-controlled distribution lists who wish to not receive *ACRONYM* e-mail may filter such mail from *ACRONYM*.

### D. Funding

1. A majority of the Senators should approve funding for an *ACRONYM* activity in a Senate Meeting prior to the event's occurrence.
2. Senators should not spend their own money to fund any *ACRONYM* activity.
3. A student representative from the group or organization at the school seeking funding should be present at a Senate Meeting to present a proposal. A written proposal should be submitted to the Senate, detailing the proposed donation request that should be approved by a majority of the Senators in a Senate Meeting.

# Appendix C: Sample Agendas

## Executive Board Meeting
## Date

I. **Call To Order**

II. **Minutes**

III. **New Business**
    A. Specific Initiative
    B. Finance Requests
    (specific requests are presented on a separate sheet listing the organization, proposed budget, and justification)

IV. **Officer Reports**
    (example of mixing the order of officer reports)
    A. **Vice President of Programming**
        i. End of term social
    B. **Executive Vice President**
        i. Bylaws amendments
    C. **Vice President of Finance**
        i. Budget update
    D. **President**
        i. Student questionnaire results
        ii. Report on meetings

V. **Breakout/Calendar Updates**

VI. **Meeting Adjournment**

## Senate Meeting Agenda
## Date
## Organization Web site URL

I. **Call To Order**

II. **Minutes**

III. **New Business**
    a. **Administrator Presentations**
       (name and title of administrator)
    b. **Finance Requests**
       (specific requests are presented on a separate sheet listing the organization, proposed budget, and justification)

IV. **Officer Reports**
    (example of formal order of officer reports)
    **A.** President (name and e-mail address)
       i. Advocacy update
       ii. Report on meetings with administrators
    **B.** Executive Vice President (name and e-mail address)
       i. Senator appreciation
    **C.** Vice President of Finance (name and e-mail address)
       i. Electronic finance request system overview
    **D.** Vice President of Academic Programs
       (name and e-mail address)
       i. Upcoming Seminar
    **E.** Vice President of Social Programs
       (name and e-mail address)
       i. Mixer details

V. **Committee Updates**
    a. Committee Chair 1 (name and e-mail address)
    b. Committee Chair 2 (name and e-mail address)
    c. Committee Chair 3 (name and e-mail address)

VI. **Senator Announcements**

VII. **Any Other Business**

VIII. **Meeting Adjournment**

# Appendix D: Time Matrix

Below is a table that can be used in scheduling meeting times and events for board or committee members. They can place an X in the time slots during the week when they are not available for reasons such as class, work, or other meeting. From this, you can determine the available time by looking at time periods when most have no X's or at least find time periods when most people are free.

**Table D: Matrix of Available Times for Scheduling**

|          | Mon | Tue | Wed | Thu | Fri |
|----------|-----|-----|-----|-----|-----|
| 9 am     |     |     |     |     |     |
| 9:30 am  |     |     |     |     |     |
| 10 am    |     |     |     |     |     |
| 10:30 am |     |     |     |     |     |
| 11 am    |     |     |     |     |     |
| 11:30 am |     |     |     |     |     |
| 12 pm    |     |     |     |     |     |
| 12:30 pm |     |     |     |     |     |
| 1 pm     |     |     |     |     |     |
| 1:30 pm  |     |     |     |     |     |
| 2 pm     |     |     |     |     |     |
| 2:30 pm  |     |     |     |     |     |
| 3 pm     |     |     |     |     |     |
| 3:30 pm  |     |     |     |     |     |
| 4 pm     |     |     |     |     |     |
| 4:30 pm  |     |     |     |     |     |
| 5 pm     |     |     |     |     |     |
| 5:30 pm  |     |     |     |     |     |
| 6 pm     |     |     |     |     |     |
| 6:30 pm  |     |     |     |     |     |
| 7 pm     |     |     |     |     |     |
| 7:30 pm  |     |     |     |     |     |
| 8 pm     |     |     |     |     |     |
| 8:30 pm  |     |     |     |     |     |
| 9 pm     |     |     |     |     |     |

# Appendix E: Sample Funding Request Form

## School Student Government/Organization
## Sample Request for Funding

Name of Student Organization: _____

Campus Address: _____

Campus Phone Number: _____

E-mail Address: _____

Web Address: _____

Date of Event: _____

Event Title: _____

Description of Event:

_____

_____

_____

_____

Number of People Expected: _____

% of Students: _____

**Event Expenses**

| Description | Amount ($) | School Vendor Code |
|---|---|---|
| | | |
| | | |
| | | |
| | | |
| | | |

Amount Requested ($): _____       Account: _____

I declare that all the above information is true to the best of my knowledge.

| | | |
|---|---|---|
| Student Org Officer's Name | Signature | Date |

# Appendix F: Sample Member Survey

## The Questionnaire

This survey is administered by the International Students Committee, a branch of [Student Organization Name]. It is intended exclusively for international students at [School Name]. The purpose of this survey is to obtain information about the needs and concerns of international students and about the students themselves. Your responses to all items in this survey will be kept confidential and will only be reported together with the responses of all other respondents. By completing this questionnaire, you agree to participate in the study.

The International Students Committee would like to thank you for your time and effort in completing this survey.

1.  Country of origin (drop-down menu)

2.  Department at [School Name] (drop-down menu)

3.  Gender
    a.  Female
    b.  Male

4.  Residence
    a.  On campus
    b.  Within 3 miles from campus
    c.  4-10 miles from campus
    d.  11-19 miles from campus
    e.  20 or more miles from campus

5.  My transition into becoming a student at [School Name] was trouble-free.

    | 1 | 2 | 3 | 4 | 5 |
    |---|---|---|---|---|
    | Strongly Agree | Agree | Neutral | Disagree | Strongly Disagree |

6.  Did you have a personal contact in the United States before you enrolled at [School Name]?
    a.  Yes
    b.  No

7. Did you stay in the United States for more than six months before you enrolled at [School Name]?
   a. Yes
   b. No

8. Indicate which of the following you had problems with during your transition to [School Name] (check all that apply):

   _ Office of International Students
   _ US Citizenship and Immigration Services
   _ Your academic department
   _ Registration
   _ International student associations
   _ [School Name] Housing
   _ Housing
   _ [School Name] Transportation
   _ Local transportation
   _ Department of Motor Vehicles (DMV)
   _ Social network/support
   _ Making friends/personal contacts
   _ Health care (e.g., insurance, student health care, etc.)
   _ Personal safety
   _ Establishing financial credit
   _ Other (explain)

9. Indicate how helpful representatives of the following services have been during your academic stay at [School Name]. Use the following scale:

| 1 | 2 | 3 | 4 | 5 |
|---|---|---|---|---|
| Strongly Agree | Agree | Neutral | Disagree | Strongly Disagree |

a. Office of International Students    1 2 3 4 5

b. US Citizenship and Immigration Services    1 2 3 4 5

c. Your academic department    1 2 3 4 5

d. Registrar's Office    1 2 3 4 5

e. International student associations    1 2 3 4 5

f. [Your Student Organization's Name]    1 2 3 4 5

g. [School Name] Transportation    1 2 3 4 5

h. Local transportation    1 2 3 4 5

i. Housing    1 2 3 4 5

j. Social life at [School Name]    1 2 3 4 5

k. Health care    1 2 3 4 5

l. Safety on and around campus    1 2 3 4 5

m. Establishing financial credit    1 2 3 4 5

10. Additional comments related to your transition to [School Name]:

## Appendix G: Sample Memorandum

(Below is a sample memorandum that is to be sent with a report to administrators.)

## Official Student Organization Letterhead Memorandum

**To:** Dr. [First & Last Name], Senior Vice President
**Cc:** Dr. [First & Last Name], Vice Provost
    Dr. [First & Last Name], Dean of International Students
    Dr. [First & Last Name], Dean of Student Life
    Chief [First & Last Name], Director of Campus Safety
**From:** [Your First & Last Name], President, [your organization]
**Date:** [Date]
**Subject:** Survey of International Students

Attached is a copy of the recent Survey of International Students at [School Name] conducted by the International Students Committee of the [Your Student Organization Name]. The survey has identified several areas of International Student life that are of concern, and with your help, the [Your Student Organization Name] would like to open a dialogue to discuss the possibility of making policy changes in these areas. While more research is ongoing into the exact nature of International Student concerns, I would appreciate the opportunity to meet with you to discuss this report and how we can all help make [School Name] a better place for all International Students.

Please feel free to contact me at [your contact number] or by e-mail at [your e-mail address] with any questions.

Attachment: International Students Committee Survey Report

# Appendix H: Sample Departmental Survey

(Below is a questionnaire that may be administered to the members.)

DIRECTIONS: Please fill out this survey using as much space as you want. Reply via e-mail to [e-mail address] by [Month Day, Year] with your completed survey.

Overall, are you satisfied with your department?
Please insert an X in one: Yes__ No__ Undecided__
Please explain your answer here.

What are the problems with your department?

What are your suggestions to improve the quality and solve the problems of your department?

What are your opinions/problems/suggestions about the curriculum in the courses?

What are your opinions/problems/suggestions about your program of study?

Please comment on anything else here about your issues and concerns.

## Appendix I: Sample Board Survey

(Below is a questionnaire that may be administered to outgoing and current board/committee members. The survey can be e-mailed or printed and given directly to them.)

Are you satisfied with this organization?
Please insert an X in one: Yes___  No___  Undecided___
Please explain your answer here.

What are the successes of this organization?

What are the problems of this organization?

What are your most important issues you think this organization should address?

What are suggestions for improvements to this organization?

Please write any additional comments here.

# References

We are grateful for the information in this book attributed to the sources listed in alphabetical order below.

*Computer Science Graduate Organization (CSGO)*, Department of Computer Science, University of Southern California, Los Angeles, California

*Future Business Leaders of America (FBLA)*, Renton High School, Renton, Washington

*Graduate and Professional Student Senate (GPSS)*, University of Southern California, Los Angeles, California

*Graduate Technology Alliance (GTA) of the Entrepreneur Venture Management Association*, Marshall School of Business, University of Southern California, Los Angeles, California

Likert, R. "A Technique for the Measurement of Attitudes," *Archives of Psychology*, 140, 55, 1932

*Merriam Webster's 11th Collegiate Dictionary*, Merriam-Webster, Incorporated, 2003

*Microsoft Office Online*, http://office.microsoft.com

Robert, Henry M., *Robert's Rules of Order*, Perseus Pub., Cambridge, MA, 2000

*USC Chapter of the American Society for Engineering Management (ASEM)*, Daniel J. Epstein Department of Industrial and Systems Engineering, University of Southern California, Los Angeles, California

*USC Chapter of the Association for Computing Machinery (ACM)*, Department of Computer Science, University of Southern California, Los Angeles, California

*Viterbi Graduate Student Association (VGSA)*, Viterbi School of Engineering, University of Southern California, Los Angeles, California

# Index

## A

action, 110
activities, 8, 13, 25, 32, 33, 38, 51, 52, 55, 56, 60, 63, 66, 78, 86, 117, 118, 120, 121, 125
activity, 14, 65, 67, 118, 125, 126
ad, 76, 111
administration, 8, 26, 37, 38, 39, 40, 43, 44, 46, 47, 75, 77, 78, 81, 82, 83, 85, 86, 87, 90, 93, 101, 103, 104
administrator, 26, 27, 60, 77, 79, 85, 86, 87, 88, 89, 90, 92, 104, 128, 153
advertisement, 57, 72, 122, 123
advertising, 57, 67
advice, 114
advisor, 9, 10, 31, 60, 66, 109, 110, 114
advocacy, 8, 13, 25, 26, 37, 38, 47, 51, 63, 75, 77, 80, 83, 85, 86, 87, 90, 91, 92, 93, 96, 99, 101, 103, 106
affiliation, 9, 11, 33, 38, 69, 114
agenda, 12, 19, 20, 21, 23, 24, 25, 26, 27, 28, 60, 63, 65, 86, 97, 122
alternative, 51, 71, 110
alumni, 32, 35, 65, 95, 103, 105, 109, 111, 117
analysis, 74, 76, 78, 79, 80
assembly, 1
association, 1, 16
award, 105, 106

## B

backup plan, 110
board, 1, 9, 10, 11, 12, 13, 14, 15, 16, 19, 20, 22, 23, 24, 27, 29, 30, 31, 32, 33, 34, 35, 36, 40, 41, 42, 43, 44, 45, 46, 47, 52, 53, 54, 55, 56, 59, 60, 63, 64, 70, 74, 76, 82, 87, 90, 91, 92, 95, 99, 101, 102, 103, 105, 108, 109, 110, 111, 112, 113, 114, 129, 141
body, 1, 5, 7, 8, 13, 18, 23, 24, 35, 38, 41, 42, 43, 45, 46, 53, 65, 77, 79, 80, 85, 89, 91, 92, 95, 97, 101, 104, 105, 113, 117, 124
brochure, 53, 67
budget, 1, 12, 13, 17, 23, 24, 37, 38, 39, 40, 41, 42, 43, 44, 45, 46, 47, 48, 51, 54, 57, 64, 67, 70, 71, 72, 73, 74, 76, 78, 82, 85, 87, 90, 91, 92, 93, 96, 103, 105, 118, 127, 128
buying, 42, 91
bylaws, 9, 24, 27, 29, 30, 31, 33, 34, 35, 36, 42, 76, 97, 98, 110, 112, 113, 114

# C

calendar, 47, 64, 88, 95

campaign, 17, 37, 95, 97, 98

candidate, 7, 13, 97, 98, 99, 121, 123, 124, 125

chair, 1, 16, 21, 22, 46, 54, 55, 60, 70, 71, 76, 82, 93, 102, 104, 112, 153

challenge, 1, 7, 14, 25, 41, 68, 69, 98, 100, 107, 112

checklist, 107

class, 1, 8, 22, 55, 67, 69, 87, 129

club, 1

comment, 21, 139

committee, 1, 10, 12, 13, 15, 16, 19, 20, 21, 22, 23, 24, 26, 27, 30, 31, 32, 34, 35, 36, 42, 44, 45, 46, 47, 51, 52, 54, 59, 60, 63, 67, 70, 71, 72, 73, 74, 75, 76, 78, 80, 82, 93, 95, 96, 104, 105, 106, 107, 109, 111, 112, 129, 141, 153

communication, 5, 7, 10, 12, 13, 15, 73, 86, 109

computer, 52, 64

concerns, 26, 70, 75, 76, 77, 81, 83, 86, 98, 107, 117, 133, 137, 139

conclusion, 79, 121, 122

conference, 15, 22, 42, 71, 72, 73

constitution, 9, 13, 24, 29, 30, 31, 32, 33, 34, 35, 36, 43, 63, 86, 97, 98, 110, 112, 113, 114

cost, 39, 40, 41, 45, 46, 51, 54, 64, 66, 67, 72, 74, 90, 91, 109, 110

council, 1

cycle, 36, 51, 75

# D

data, 75, 76, 77, 78, 79, 80, 81, 82, 91

decision, 7, 10, 40, 45, 47, 82, 85, 86, 99, 101, 112, 121

demotion, 111

director, 17, 60, 76

discussion, 20, 22, 24, 44, 76, 79, 80, 81, 117

dismiss, 112

document, 20, 30, 31, 32, 36, 75, 82, 102, 104

dress, 87, 128

duties, 11, 29, 34, 96, 112, 119

# E

election, 17, 33, 37, 41, 86, 87, 95, 96, 97, 98, 99, 101, 102, 113, 124, 125

e-mail, 3, 5, 7, 9, 13, 16, 22, 30, 46, 51, 52, 53, 54, 55, 56, 57, 64, 67, 68, 69, 70, 71, 72, 73, 78, 88, 91, 96, 112, 118, 119, 122, 123, 124, 125, 128, 137, 139, 141

employee, 41

event, 21, 32, 42, 43, 44, 45, 46, 53, 57, 58, 59, 63, 64, 65, 66, 67, 68, 69, 70, 71, 73, 74, 92, 105, 123, 126

expenditure, 43

## F

factor, 24, 103, 108, 109

faculty, 9, 26, 65, 66, 72, 78, 87, 96, 125

fee, 37, 38, 39, 40, 41, 43, 44, 67, 70, 72

feedback, 31, 36, 60, 63, 72, 73, 74, 76, 98, 107, 108, 109, 111, 115

finance, 12, 13, 20, 23, 24, 27, 44, 45, 46, 47, 128

flyer, 53, 67

food, 16, 23, 26, 39, 41, 46, 57, 58, 59, 60, 66, 68, 70, 71, 73, 74, 97, 99, 101, 105

form, 1, 8, 9, 12, 24, 28, 32, 41, 43, 47, 69, 77, 78, 79, 99, 101, 105, 108, 111, 114, 115

formula, 57, 58

funding, 17, 25, 28, 39, 45, 46, 47, 64, 66, 67, 121, 123, 126

## G

game, 14, 65, 112

government, 1, 3, 8, 9, 10, 12, 13, 17, 20, 26, 29, 31, 32, 34, 37, 38, 39, 41, 42, 43, 45, 46, 47, 55, 59, 60, 75, 95, 97, 111, 123, 153

group, 1, 5, 6, 7, 8, 9, 10, 11, 12, 13, 14, 15, 16, 18, 19, 25, 26, 28, 29, 30, 32, 33, 34, 35, 38, 39, 42, 43, 45, 47, 51, 52, 53, 54, 55, 56, 60, 61, 63, 65, 66, 67, 69, 70, 72, 80, 89, 93, 95, 96, 100, 101, 103, 104, 108, 111, 113, 114, 117, 126

## H

honorarium, 41, 72

## I

identify, 81, 107, 108, 109

imbalance, 31, 32, 44

impact, 9, 54, 69, 71, 78, 95, 109, 110, 115

improve, 15, 23, 30, 31, 36, 37, 45, 63, 73, 76, 81, 90, 95, 107, 113, 139

improvement, 1, 39, 93, 111, 114

income, 5, 39, 40, 44

institution, 5, 9, 13, 66, 75, 81, 82, 85, 88, 90, 93, 106, 113, 114

issues, 9, 10, 13, 14, 16, 17, 19, 20, 21, 22, 25, 31, 44, 47, 60, 67, 75, 76, 78, 81, 82, 83, 85, 87, 88, 93, 95, 99, 102, 103, 104, 107, 109, 110, 113, 121, 139, 141

# L

leader, 1, 5, 6, 7, 8, 10, 12, 14, 15, 16, 17, 23, 24, 25, 26, 27, 28, 30, 32, 34, 37, 38, 41, 42, 45, 47, 53, 65, 75, 76, 77, 81, 82, 85, 86, 87, 88, 90, 92, 93, 103, 104, 105, 109, 110, 111, 112, 113, 114, 115

leadership, 1, 5, 6, 9, 10, 11, 12, 15, 16, 18, 27, 29, 31, 34, 63, 73, 76, 77, 86, 92, 93, 95, 96, 99, 100, 101, 102, 103, 104, 106, 111, 112, 113, 114, 115, 153

leading, 1, 14, 35, 44, 74, 99, 107

letter, 6, 92, 99

liaison, 117

life, 1, 7, 8, 14, 16, 18, 23, 37, 39, 54, 65, 75, 78, 79, 81, 87, 88, 90, 93, 95, 103, 112, 135, 137

list, 13, 21, 55, 56, 57, 68, 79, 87, 96, 100, 104, 109, 121, 123

logo, 53, 54, 93, 100

# M

mail, 13, 16, 51, 52, 54, 56, 78, 118, 122, 125, 131, 137, 139

management, 6, 66, 70

meeting, 8, 15, 19, 20, 21, 22, 23, 24, 25, 26, 27, 28, 36, 46, 53, 59, 60, 63, 85, 86, 87, 88, 89, 92, 93, 96, 97, 100, 102, 118, 121, 122, 129

member, 1, 9, 12, 13, 21, 28, 32, 33, 54, 59, 67, 70, 72, 96, 100, 102, 105, 112, 122, 124

membership, 9, 14, 24, 34, 35, 39, 55, 63, 65, 67, 97, 111, 112, 114, 117, 119

memorandum, 137

method, 25, 55, 91

minutes, 20, 22, 26, 46, 55, 76, 100, 105, 106, 118, 121

mission, 1, 3, 32, 51, 103

money, 6, 13, 21, 24, 27, 37, 38, 39, 41, 42, 43, 44, 45, 47, 54, 61, 63, 64, 67, 73, 74, 90, 91, 104, 125, 126

morale, 12, 111

# N

newspaper, 67, 72, 82, 99

# O

objective, 32, 75, 117

office, 13, 14, 15, 16, 17, 33, 34, 37, 39, 41, 42, 47, 54, 59, 72, 79, 82, 87, 89, 96, 98, 100, 103, 104, 112, 119, 143

officer, 1, 9, 12, 13, 15, 16, 20, 21, 23, 24, 25, 27, 33, 40, 41, 42, 44, 45, 47, 51, 54, 55, 59, 60, 66, 67, 68, 70, 71, 93, 95, 96, 99, 101, 102, 104, 106, 119, 127, 128 option, 98, 109

organization, 1, 5, 6, 7, 8, 9, 10, 11, 12, 13, 14, 15, 16, 17, 18, 20, 21, 22, 23, 24, 26, 27, 28, 29, 30, 31, 32, 33, 34, 35, 36, 37, 38, 39, 43, 45, 46, 47, 51, 52, 53, 54, 55, 56, 57, 59, 60, 61, 63, 64, 65, 66, 67, 68, 69, 70, 72, 73, 74, 76, 77, 78, 79, 80, 81, 82, 85, 87, 90, 93, 95, 96, 97, 98, 99, 100, 102, 103, 104, 105, 106, 107, 108, 109, 110, 111, 112, 113, 114, 115, 117, 120, 126, 127, 128, 137, 141

orientation, 53, 55, 67, 100, 101

# P

parliamentary, 22

partnership, 72, 83, 89, 92, 93, 105

performance, 111

phone, 6, 7, 41, 59

policy, 19, 34, 37, 42, 65, 75, 76, 78, 81, 85, 88, 89, 93, 106, 137

poll, 65

position, 6, 7, 11, 12, 13, 15, 16, 23, 26, 29, 32, 33, 37, 38, 58, 96, 98, 99, 101, 102, 104, 112, 114, 117, 118, 119, 121, 123, 124, 125

president, 12, 13, 16, 17, 23, 24, 25, 27, 32, 34, 60, 66, 82, 88, 97, 98, 99, 100, 101, 103, 104, 106, 153

prioritize, 6, 7, 87, 109

probation, 113

problem, 6, 24, 56, 75, 77, 78, 81, 87, 98, 102, 107, 110, 113

process, 1, 6, 7, 9, 14, 29, 30, 31, 35, 45, 46, 47, 86, 95, 96, 97, 99, 101, 106, 107, 111, 112, 113, 114, 119

program, 32, 43, 60, 63, 64, 66, 67, 69, 71, 74, 77, 104, 105, 139

programming, 13, 23, 25, 33, 37, 38, 39, 40, 41, 42, 43, 44, 46, 47, 63, 64, 66, 67, 68, 70, 71, 74, 85, 93, 96

promotional items, 54, 55

public relations, 54, 55, 57, 93, 96, 105, 106

publicity, 51, 54, 61, 66, 67, 72, 76, 93

purchase, 16, 46, 54, 57, 93, 123

purchase order, 123

# Q

quality, 3, 23, 30, 37, 39, 73, 88, 93, 103, 139

# R

recognition, 9, 14, 30, 31, 34, 43, 105, 113

recommendation, 6, 44

recruitment, 76, 95, 96

regulation, 29

report, 24, 43, 71, 76, 79, 80, 81, 82, 83, 88, 92, 93, 103, 104, 105, 121, 137

representation, 8, 27, 31, 95, 101

representative, 26, 27, 28, 46, 60, 77, 85, 86, 91, 105, 124, 126

reputation, 7, 16, 53, 65, 66, 74, 81, 90, 92, 111

request, 21, 24, 28, 38, 43, 45, 46, 47, 86, 91, 126, 128

requisition, 47

reservation, 97

resource, 1, 103

response, 16, 20, 37, 76, 77, 78, 79, 80, 88, 93, 110, 122

responsibilities, 1, 6, 20, 29, 31, 32, 41, 66, 81, 96, 100, 101, 102, 112, 113, 115, 123

restructuring, 113

result, 1, 5, 6, 25, 46, 58, 81, 89, 90, 91, 107, 110, 113

reward, 14, 25, 111

risk, 29, 52, 65, 66, 90, 91

RSVP, 64, 74, 105

rule, 29


# S

salary, 40, 41

sanction, 61

satisfaction, 74

scale, 10, 40, 64, 77, 82, 108, 109, 135

schedule, 25, 60, 64, 67, 68, 69, 72, 73, 76, 89

school, 6, 8, 9, 10, 13, 15, 16, 17, 19, 23, 25, 26, 30, 31, 32, 33, 34, 36, 37, 38, 39, 42, 43, 44, 45, 46, 47, 51, 52, 53, 54, 55, 56, 57, 59, 60, 61, 63, 64, 65, 66, 67, 68, 69, 70, 71, 72, 75, 77, 78, 79, 80, 81, 82, 85, 86, 87, 88, 89, 90, 92, 93, 95, 96, 97, 99, 100, 102, 103, 104, 105, 106, 110, 111, 123, 124, 125, 126, 153

senate, 10, 24, 25, 26, 27, 31, 32, 33, 36, 39, 40, 42, 43, 44, 45, 47, 54, 60, 63, 76, 82, 87, 91, 92, 97, 98, 99, 103, 105

senator, 12, 25, 26, 27, 105, 153

society, 1, 9

software, 53, 54

speaker, 60, 72, 106

special election, 33, 113

speech, 17, 97, 98

staff, 9, 12, 13, 17, 18, 23, 39, 41, 55, 65, 66, 70, 73, 109, 110, 111, 123, 125

statement, 17, 32, 51, 82, 96, 103

steps, 1, 29, 35, 113

storage, 15, 16, 41

student, 1, 3, 5, 6, 7, 8, 9, 10, 11, 12, 13, 14, 15, 16, 17, 18, 19, 20, 23, 24, 25, 26, 27, 28, 29, 30, 31, 32, 34, 35, 36, 37, 38, 39, 40, 41, 42, 43, 44, 45, 46, 47, 52, 53, 54, 55, 59, 60, 63, 65, 66, 67, 68, 69, 71, 75, 77, 78, 79, 80, 81, 82, 85, 86, 87, 88, 89, 90, 91, 92, 93, 95, 97, 98, 99, 101, 102, 103, 104, 106, 110, 111, 113, 114, 115, 117, 120, 123, 124, 125, 126, 133, 134, 135, 153

student organization leadership, 1

success, 1, 12, 15, 17, 63, 64, 65, 66, 67, 71, 74, 85, 87, 88, 90, 91, 92, 93, 101, 105, 110, 115

supplies, 6, 16, 41, 46, 58, 59, 69

survey, 73, 76, 77, 78, 80, 81, 82, 91, 108, 133, 137, 139, 141


**T**

tabling, 55, 97

task force, 76, 111

team, 10, 12, 14, 30, 73, 76, 99, 100, 101, 109, 111, 112

technology, 76

term, 5, 11, 12, 15, 25, 33, 43, 44, 51, 55, 59, 64, 65, 67, 75, 86, 87, 91, 92, 93, 96, 101, 102, 113, 119, 122, 123, 124, 127

tickets, 67, 123, 125

time, 6, 7, 8, 9, 11, 12, 13, 15, 17, 18, 19, 20, 21, 22, 23, 24, 25, 28, 29, 30, 33, 36, 37, 40, 41, 42, 44, 45, 46, 53, 54, 55, 56, 59, 60, 64, 67, 69, 70, 71, 72, 73, 74, 76, 78, 79, 80, 82, 86, 88, 89, 90, 92, 93, 95, 96, 97, 98, 99, 100, 101, 102, 104, 105, 106, 109, 113, 121, 122, 123, 124, 125, 129, 133

training, 1, 6, 16, 102

transition, 81, 87, 96, 99, 100, 102, 106, 112, 113, 114, 133, 134, 135

transportation, 39, 69, 91, 134, 135


**V**

vacancy, 32

vendor, 23, 47, 57

venue, 67, 69, 70, 71, 72, 73, 74, 105

vice president, 12, 13, 16, 17, 23, 33, 86, 98, 102, 153

vision, 14, 17, 19, 24, 41, 60, 61, 90, 100, 101, 103, 106

volunteer, 11, 14, 16, 44, 105

vote, 20, 21, 22, 24, 25, 27, 28, 31, 34, 36, 40, 43, 44, 45, 46, 82, 97, 98, 99, 102, 105, 118, 119, 121, 124, 125

voting, 17, 22, 24, 25, 32, 45, 46, 75, 96, 97, 98, 121, 124


**W**

Web site, 1, 9, 13, 17, 31, 36, 45, 51, 52, 53, 54, 56, 57, 60, 64, 67, 70, 72, 93, 96, 97, 99, 108, 115, 118, 123, 128 work, 6, 7, 11, 12, 13, 14, 15, 16, 17, 19, 21, 22, 23, 26, 33, 40, 52, 57, 66, 73, 75, 76, 78, 80, 81, 85, 89, 90, 91, 93, 96, 102, 105, 110, 111, 112, 129

# About the Authors

## Biography of Cyrus Fakharzadeh

Born, educated, and raised in the United States, Cyrus has a Bachelor's degree from the University of Washington in Seattle and two Master's degrees (one in Engineering Management) from the University of Southern California. Additionally, he completed an MS degree with a Master's Thesis from the New York Institute of Technology in Old Westbury. A certified Project Management Professional from the Project Management Institute, he attained a Project Management Certificate from the California Institute of Technology; and he has been working as a manager for a number of years. With five years of experience as a president of high school and college student organizations, he has five years of experience as a vice president, senator, and committee chair. He has achieved numerous high school and college leadership awards for his service and contributions to a variety of student groups; and he has been consulting for numerous student groups and leaders for many years.

## Biography of Mark Todd

Mark was raised in Ireland, earning a Bachelor's degree from the University of Ulster and a Master's degree from The Queen's University of Belfast, Northern Ireland. He holds a Ph.D. from the University of Southern California where he currently works as an administrator. He has four years experience in graduate student government having held the positions of committee chair, vice president, and president; and he serves as a mentor to graduate student leaders at the university. Mark is married with three children and lives in Los Angeles, California.